ALL YOU NEED TO KNOW ABOUT HEAVEN

All you need
to know about
Heaven

A biblical exploration

GUY CHAPMAN

THANKFUL BOOKS

Copyright © Guy Chapman 2007

First published 2007

Published by Thankful Books,
c/o P.O. Box 2118, Seaford, BN25 9AR.

ISBN 978 1 905084 12 8

Book design and production for the publisher by
Bookprint Creative Services, <www.bookprint.co.uk>
Printed in Great Britain.

With loving thanks to my daughter
Rachel Wigram
for her support and wise counsel

Contents

Preface

This book owes its origin to some friends who, having read my earlier book, *All You Need to Know About Hell*, suggested that I ought to balance it with another about heaven. In that earlier book I did my best to look at every text that might have any bearing on the subject, and yet I am aware that from the outset I had a definite agenda, my aim was to speak out against a particular understanding which I believed to be unbiblical, and to present an alternative which I believed to be biblical. This second book has no such agenda. My object has been simply to look at all the Scriptures and see where they led me, and to try to bring together the totality of the biblical revelation. Where I have come across ideas that I have thought to be wrong I have endeavoured to give a clear reason for my decisions, and yet ultimately the line I have taken is not so much that certain ideas are necessarily wrong, but that because I cannot see how they can be made to fit in with all the rest of the evidence I personally will have to discount them. Two issues in particular caused me considerable difficulty, but my understanding grew as I wrestled with them. Overall the problems were relatively few, and the majority of my study has been a positive and joyful experience.

The subject is so vast, and so far beyond our ability to comprehend, that there are bound to be some differences of understanding. As I say at one point, 'There is as little chance of us ever understanding some of these things in this life, as there is of a dog trying to understand how a computer works; our understanding may not get beyond that of the poor dog wagging his tail.' but I hope that this effort will rekindle in some a vision of a glory that far transcends all earthly glories, and that our hearts may be lifted up in worship and adoration, and of course, eager anticipation.

Guy Chapman

PROLOGUE

'But I Don't Like That!'

For Tom it had been a perfectly normal sort of day. He had got up at the usual time, had his usual breakfast – muesli, half a grapefruit, toast and marmalade. He had kissed his wife goodbye and gone to work. At work he had felt no need to exert himself, he was coming up to retirement and there seemed little point in launching out on any new project, it was just a matter of keeping on top of the ordinary routine stuff. He had returned home, had supper, finished the crossword he had started at breakfast, watched a pleasant little nature programme on television, and gone to bed. He hadn't anticipated that would be the last day of his life here on earth, but here he was now in heaven.

Well, he assumed it was heaven. He had seen nothing to indicate that it was, but it couldn't be the 'other place', it was much too nice for that. Why he had died, and how he had got there he didn't know, all he knew was that he was there.

At first he was so taken up with finding himself in this unexpected situation that he hardly noticed the other people around him, but after a time he began to realise that he was far from alone, there were other people everywhere. He decided he had better do a bit of exploring, after all, if this was heaven, he supposed he was going to be there for

11

a long time – he had never quite understood the idea of eternity, but it sounded like a very long time indeed.

It wasn't long, however, before he began to be troubled. These other people – they seemed to be very like people he'd known on earth. There was a group in one place playing loud music of a type he didn't appreciate. He had always defended the right of people to like that sort of music, if they really wanted to, but surely it wouldn't be found in heaven?

In another place he came upon what seemed to be a party with plenty of food that was free for anyone who wished to join in. Up until then he hadn't thought about food and he was puzzled because he didn't think that anyone would actually need to eat in heaven. He was even more puzzled when someone offered him a plate of ox eyes. A person from somewhere like Outer Mongolia might have looked upon that as a delicacy, but his stomach churned at the mere sight of it. Surely you wouldn't find that sort of stuff in heaven? And were there really oxen in heaven, and did they farm them for food? And finally, could you really have a stomach that churned in heaven?

He became increasingly agitated until he began to run about wildly, but wherever he turned, he found things that disturbed him. In desperation he called out, 'I would rather be sitting on a cloud, playing a harp.' And there he was, up on a cloud, with this great big harp. He couldn't even play the piano, far less a harp, and he felt a complete idiot.

'I didn't mean it.' He shouted. 'It was just a joke.'

He was immediately engulfed by laughter, laughter everywhere, laughter so loud that his cloud began to shake. He dropped his harp. He was about to fall. He screamed but still the shaking went on, shaking, shaking, shaking.

*   *   *

With a jolt he woke up, to find his wife shaking him. 'For goodness sake wake up.' She was saying. 'You've been calling out again and again, "But I don't like that!" And then you began to scream.'

'But I thought I was in heaven.' He said.

'Heaven? It sounded more like hell to me! Now, for goodness sake, settle down, I would like to get some sleep.'

For Tom, more sleep was impossible until he had done some serious thinking. Obviously his nightmare had brought together all sorts of half-formed questions about heaven that he had pushed into the back of his mind. What few thoughts he did have on the subject were clearly ridiculous, but what was the truth?

Was there really such a place? Or was it a state of existence? What would it really be like? When he did actually die, would he go there, would he be part of it? How could he find any sensible answers – all he generally heard on the subject seemed to be rather silly stories, though few had been as silly as his nightmare. He wondered whether he should ask the vicar about it, but he was afraid of being thought to be an ignorant fool. He didn't know the vicar very well and saw him as a rather threatening figure, who might not take kindly to being asked difficult questions by someone who didn't normally bother to come to listen to his sermons.

Eventually he resolved that he would secretly get out the old Bible that he had been given when he had gone to a Sunday School. He knew where it was because he had sought it out that very evening to find the answer to a rather obscure crossword clue – perhaps it was that which had triggered his dream. Well, he would see if it might give him any answers. With that thought he fell asleep at last; and with that thought began a quest that was to change his life for ever.

1

A Plan for the Journey

When setting out on any journey it is wise to have a plan. Events may lead to alterations along the way, but if we have no plan at all we may well end up not getting anywhere in particular. That may not matter all that much if it is just a recreational stroll; but we are on a precise mission – we wish to learn, as best we can, what the Bible teaches about heaven – we need a plan.

It is also a wise precaution to make a preliminary investigation of the possible route to see if there are any obvious problems to be expected, or diversions that will need to be taken. A preliminary investigation of our particular trip through the Bible, points to five questions that we will eventually want to answer; questions that could be summarised as, Where? What? When? Who? and How?

Who will be in heaven and what will they be like, how will they get there and when? What exactly is heaven, and where will it be? The answer to that last question may seem obvious, heaven will be in heaven! But we will find that there are big issues to be faced, and these together with equally large questions about when, will require us to explore two complicated diversions before we can reach the end of our journey. Some may decide that they would prefer to bypass the diversion relating to the millennium, but the other diversion may show us such unexpected delights and lead us to such important truths that it would be a shame to miss it.

How can we best prepare for our particular journey? The critical word is 'consistency'. On the one hand we need to realise that we are dealing with the words and works of someone who is always consistent. God is consistent. The God of the New Testament is the same as the God of the Old Testament, and the God of the book of Revelation is the same as the God of the rest of the New Testament. There is, of course, development as we move through the Bible, more is revealed as we go along, but while new things may be revealed, that which is revealed is always consistent with what has gone before. We will therefore start by looking at what we can find in the foundational early chapters, Genesis 1–3. We will then move on to the rest of the Old Testament. After that we will come to the Gospels, then the Epistles, and finally Revelation. At each stage we will try to keep in mind that nothing that is said will contradict what has been said earlier.

On the other hand if God's revelation in the Scriptures is consistent, we for our part must also be consistent in the way that we use them. We will need to prayerfully decide which parts are plain statements of fact, and which parts are inspired illustrations. Generally this is quite clear, but there are a few places where we will have to think carefully before making a decision. What is not consistent, and therefore not allowable, is to take most of a passage as an illustration but to pluck out a few verses from it and say that these bits are factual. Approaching the consistent Scriptures in a consistent manner will be crucial in reaching reliable conclusions.

As already said we will have to make some major diversions to try to sort out some problems about when and where? Then we will be ready to try to take stock of all we have found, and make some final decisions.

The process of working all through the Bible may at times seem tedious, and some may prefer to give it a miss and go straight to the conclusions as presented in Chapter 22, but it is to be hoped that if you do this you may later want to come back to the earlier chapters to check the evidence that leads to those conclusions.

To reach the right conclusions it will be important that we have all the evidence. In particular, to go straight to the book of Revelation, without first working through the rest of the Bible, is likely to lead us to seriously distorted conclusions. In all of this we should be clear that we need to avoid the danger of looking for a few 'proof verses' that will 'prove' what we want to be proved, instead we need to do our utmost to discover all that God has revealed on the subject, whether it agrees with our original ideas, or turns them upside down. There are far too many ideas around that are based on a few proof texts while ignoring all the rest.

When I started working on this book I thought I already had a good biblical understanding of the subject, but a deeper study of all the evidence showed me that there was much that I still needed to learn and that some of my ideas needed to be changed considerably. Some parts of my original script had to be revised many times as my understanding developed and before I could reach what seemed to me to be a reasonable harmony of all the biblical material. I guess that I am far from unique in this, and that the probability is that on this subject we all have things we need to learn, or unlearn, or relearn.

If you personally find the information gathering too tedious you may prefer to 'sleep' through the early part of the journey, but in one way or another I invite you to travel with me, you may find that your ideas are reinforced, or perhaps like mine they will be changed for the better. We are certainly heading for an amazing destination. It is a journey well worth making.

2

Basic Geography

When looking at the word 'heaven' we need to be clear what we are talking about, and this is not always straightforward because the word can mean widely different things. My dictionary gives several different meanings. First there are what we more normally call the sky; any particular scientific, or imaginary, ring of atmosphere around the earth; and space in general, all of which could be described as purely 'geographical'. Secondly it can mean the dwelling-place of God, or the gods; and of angelic hosts and those blessed to be there. And thirdly, a less often used meaning, as a name for God himself, being the one who inhabits it. And finally there are all the 'spin-offs', by which I mean the use of the word to mean anything very good, such as when we describe something as 'pure heaven'.

While the one word can be used in all these different ways, we do, at least in the English language, have alternatives that we can use, such as 'sky' and 'space'. In both the Hebrew of the Old Testament and the Greek of the New Testament, the situation is more confusing because in both languages there is only the one word for all the possible different meanings. Both the Hebrew *shamayim* and the Greek *ouranos* mean both the sky and anything 'above,' and God's dwelling place.

In Psalm 89 another word is twice used for the sky, but this is insignificant compared with the more than three hundred uses of *shamayim*.

Twice in Acts and six times in Revelation a compound form of the word is used, but they add nothing to the general meaning of the other more than two hundred and thirty uses of *ouranos*.

All of which may be of little interest to most readers, but it does leave us with a caution – there is nothing in the script of either the Old or New Testaments to indicate when it is speaking about the sky and when it is speaking about God's dwelling-place. We need to be careful that we do not start applying things that refer to the sky or to space, to what we normally mean by heaven. Though the word 'heaven' comes well over 550 times in the King James Version of the Bible, very few of the references are to what we would think of as the subject of this book, and this becomes apparent right from the opening chapter of Genesis.

We do not need to be over worried about this, as in practice many of the passages of Scripture that teach us most about what we call heaven do not use the word at all! But it is as well to be clear in our minds, before we start to look at the Bible, that the vast majority of verses that use the word heaven in the older translations are not about what we call heaven at all.

3

Genesis 1 – 3

Something can be found that is relevant to almost everything that is important in life in the first three chapters of
Genesis. They paint the backcloth against which the whole
saga of life is played out. What do they say about heaven?

The very first verse says, 'In the beginning when God
created the heavens and the earth.' What 'heavens' are
these that are being spoken of? The truth of the matter is
that no one can be sure, but it is most likely that it means
the sky. This account is going to be about this world and
the sky above. Alternatively it is possible that it refers to
the vastness of space, in which case it is saying that God
made everything and in particular the earth which will be
the centre of attention in this book of Genesis. What is
almost certain is that it does not mean what we normally
mean when we use the word heaven. It is not about the
subject of this book.

We may well think that looking at this first verse in the
Bible has got us nowhere, but I include it to demonstrate
what has just been said in the previous chapter about
taking care not to jump to the wrong conclusions when we
look at verses that use this word – heaven. By contrast we
will actually find more that may be relevant to the subject

in Genesis 2:15 – 3:24 even though the word for heaven/
sky doesn't come in them at all.

Perhaps the biggest question arising from these chapters
about creation that has a direct bearing on the topic of
heaven, is whether men and women, created in the image
of God, have eternal life.

Genesis 1:26–27 tell us in very definite terms that God
created men and women in his own image, that much is
absolutely clear, what is not so clear is what it actually
means. What we can surely say is that men and women
were created to possess something that other animals do
not have, but what is it? What is the exact nature of the
'image of God in man'?

Some would say it is something as basic as conscience.
Others would go much further and say that it includes
having eternal life. We need to be honest and admit that
Genesis does not make this clear. We may assume it, but
only because we are reading into it thoughts that come
from later in the Bible.

If we are inclined to say that the image of God must
include having eternal life, there is another division of
ideas, for some argue that as originally created men and
women were meant to live physically for ever.

In one way this idea can all be made to tie up neatly
together, in particular it makes Genesis 5 very poignant
with its repeated refrain at the end of each life story, 'and
he died' except in the case of the godly Enoch. However,
the straightforward meaning of Genesis 2:17, 'for in the day
that you eat of it you shall die.' is that the death would
occur on the day that the eating took place, and it has to be
said that it is hardly likely that Adam dying physically at
the age of 930 is to be seen as the penalty for something he
did wrong 900 years before. Moreover there are other very

considerable problems to the idea. In looking at this we will bring in some information that comes from much later in the Bible, but much of the information we need comes from these three chapters of Genesis, so this is the simplest place to consider it; and in considering the topic of heaven, which is clearly related to eternal life, it will be helpful to be as clear as possible from the start, what sort of eternal life we are talking about.

Firstly, the Bible nowhere says that man was originally meant to live for ever physically, if people want to believe that, it is only a supposition with no biblical support.

Secondly, we are told that God created plants and trees bearing seeds (Genesis 1:11), establishing the pattern of growth and reproduction. He similarly created living creatures and birds to multiply (1:22). Finally he created mankind to be fruitful and multiply (1:28). Such a plan demands the sort of system that we know all too well, of birth, growth, procreation, and eventual physical death. Anything that reproduces but never dies will lead to the eventual complete suffocation of any physical creation. I would contend that the curse of the Fall (when man and woman acted against the expressly stated, and clearly understood, will of God) was spiritual death, but that physical death was written into the system of this world from the very start by God himself. Physical death is not to be seen as a curse but as an integral part of God's original plan for physical life.

It is true that Hebrews 2:14 tells us that the devil 'has the power of death', but the more precise nature of this power is pointed to in the following verse which speaks of people being 'held in slavery by the fear of death', and is made even clearer in Hebrews 9:27, 'it is appointed unto mortals to die once, and after that the judgement.' Putting together all that is said, the teaching of Hebrews is that all people are mortal and will die; this is a divine appointment that need not be feared. What is to be feared is what it may lead to, namely the judgment – when we have not found peace with God.

Thirdly, Paul speaks of people who are dead in trespasses and sin when they are still very much alive physically, which indicates that the death that has come on people because of sin is not physical but spiritual. And with this it may be helpful to point out that this Paul, who in one passage in Romans 8 might seem to be speaking in favour of a literal new earth, says very definitely in other places that the hope of the Christian is that he or she will put on a new spiritual body. When we later come to look at Paul's teaching we will come across this time and time again.

Personally, I am convinced that men and women were created to have eternal spiritual life, and that it was this that was lost at the Fall, and that this is what was restored and made available once more by the death of Jesus Christ, though we may later find that 'spiritual life' is to be thought of as more like 'physical life' than we expected.

From these rather incomplete thoughts which have, as yet, an inadequate foundation, we turn to something much more clearly demonstrated in Genesis 2:15–3:24, the relationship between God and the people he had created. We may start with 2:15–17,

The LORD God took the man and put him in the garden of Eden to till it and keep it. And the Lord God commanded the man, 'You may freely eat of every tree of the garden; but of the tree of the knowledge of good and evil you shall not eat, for in the day that you eat of it you shall die.'

We will not argue here over how, literally or symbolically, we are meant to take this; it is the teaching it gives that we are concerned with. It teaches us that God cares for his created beings and provides for their welfare, but that this requires co-operation, for they are to till the land, not just eat what it produces. Further it teaches us that there is a moral dimension to their relationship, for there is at least one thing they must not do. They were not morally neutral, unable to do wrong because there was nothing proscribed as being wrong; they were morally involved, able to obey or to disobey. In other words they had the gift of free will. This gift that could be very costly as they were to discover at the Fall; was at the same time one of priceless value, because without it there could not be a relationship of love. From all of this we may deduce that God longs to have a relationship of friendship with the people he has created. We may see a further expression of this in Genesis 3:8, 'They heard the sound of the Lord God walking in the garden at the time of the evening breeze.' In these words and in the verses that follow we see a God who stoops to take a form in which he can enjoy a walk with his friends. Many see in this what may be called a 'pre-incarnation' appearance of Christ; in other words God appearing in human form to meet people at their own level, as he was eventually to do supremely in the birth, life, death and res-urrection of Jesus Christ. For our purposes the important point is that God appears to want a relationship with people, a partnership with them, and that it should be a relationship of friendship.

And now we look more fully at the tragic situation that the Fall has led to death, for God had said, Genesis 2:17, 'for in the day that you eat of it you shall die.' This I per-sonally think refers to spiritual death, for they were still

physically alive, but had clearly lost something from that
point on, the nature of which we see in Genesis 3:22–24,

> Then the LORD God said, 'See, the man has become like one of
> us, knowing good and evil; and now, he might reach out his
> hand and take also from the tree of life, and eat, and live for
> ever' – therefore the LORD God sent him forth from the garden
> of Eden, to till the ground from which he was taken. He drove
> out the man; and at the east of the garden of Eden he placed
> the cherubim, and a sword flaming and turning to guard the
> way to the tree of life.

Clearly man and woman do not now have that sort of life
that will enable them to live for ever. An intriguing point is
that it seems that there is a danger that people might try to
gain, or regain, that eternal life by the wrong means, and
some may see in this a pointer to all man-made forms of
religion. But there is also the very important point that the
tree of life is still there, which surely implies that the way
to eternal life is still available, but it must be obtained in the
right way only. This tree of life reappears in the heart of the
heavenly city in the book of Revelation, which underlines
why all of this is relevant to the subject of heaven. These
references to the tree of life, right at the start of the Bible
and again right at the end, could be taken to suggest that
throughout the Bible we can see how God has been
working to overcome the curse brought by the misuse of
free-will, until at last that gift of free-will, combined with
the grace of God, can lead to the blessing of eternal life
based on a relationship of love.

So, there is more to think over from these first chapters
of the Bible than we might have expected – they give us the
backcloth against which the saga of life will be acted out. A

backcloth that has painted on it things that indicate that God cares for the people he has made, that he wants a relationship of friendship with them (a friendship that will later be more fully defined as love), but that it must be a relationship based on free-will. There are things on that backcloth that suggest that there will be a way to eternal life, but it must be by the right way that will eventually be revealed. There are good grounds to think that this eternal life is of a spiritual nature. And all of this can lead us to look forward to what we call heaven where, according to Revelation 22:2, the tree of life grows in abundance, free for all to take its fruit and leaves, and with no cherubim or flaming sword to keep anyone away. These primary chapters do not tell us anything directly about heaven but they lay a foundation on which later revelation can be seen to sit logically and securely.

4

The Rest of the Old Testament

We have spent some time on Genesis 1–3 partly because it is foundational to all that is in the Bible, and partly because there is very little more to find on the subject anywhere else in the Old Testament. However here are three topics that have some relevance.

The first may seem somewhat negative. The Old Testament is very vague about life after death. When people die they go to Sheol (the same as Hades in the New Testament), which can be described quite simply as the place, or state, to which dead people go. There is expressed a fear of the judgment to come, and there is also a suggestion of something better for the righteous. It is a place of waiting for something, but it is not until the New Testament that we get much indication of what that something is. There are a number of places where it comes tantalisingly close to saying something, but then stops short at a hint of a reward for the righteous, or of something better.

As examples of this we may quote Genesis 5:24, 'Enoch walked with God; then he was no more, because God took him.'

'Took him where?' we may ask, and we will probably

29

think that God took him to be with himself. We may in fact be convinced that this is what it means, and yet it tantalisingly doesn't actually tell us. Or we can look at a number of passages in the Psalms, for example Psalm 73:23–25, 'Nevertheless I am continually with you; you hold my right hand. You guide me with your counsel, and afterwards you will receive me with honour. Whom have I in heaven but you? And there is nothing on earth I desire other than you.'

'After what will he be received where?' we may ask, and we will probably think that after death he will be received into heaven. We may in fact be convinced that this is what it means, and we may prefer the translation 'receive me to glory' (which is a perfectly legitimate translation) but it tantalisingly doesn't make it clear. Or we may think of that most favourite of Psalms: Psalm 23:6, 'Surely goodness and mercy shall follow me all the days of my life, and I shall dwell in the house of the Lord my whole life long.' We may throw up our hands in horror and say that we don't like that translation, it ought to be, 'for ever.' Surely David is saying that God will look after him all the days of this life and then he will go on to be with the Lord for ever? Well, yes, it could mean that, we may be convinced that it means that, but tantalisingly the original is a bit ambiguous. There are many such references throughout the Old Testament, but none can be found that actually proves the doctrine of going to heaven. What we may perhaps say is that there seems to be an attempt to lay hold of something that had not yet been fully revealed. What we have is not proof of the reality of heaven to come, but things that point to the possibility and prepare us for the revelation when it comes.

The second point is to do with angels. These appear only occasionally but are mentioned in seventeen of the books of the Old Testament. There are times when 'the angel of the

Lord' could be taken to be God himself appearing in a form that men and women can comprehend, a Christ-like figure; though others think this is more likely to be an angel vested with the full authority of God to act on his behalf. But there are also other angels that definitely cannot be taken to be an appearance of God himself.

The first clear mention of an angel comes in Genesis 16:7–14 where 'The angel of the Lord' appears to Hagar. What is not so clear is whether this means God himself showing himself in human form, or whether this is an entity apart from God. But when we look at the second mention in Genesis 18 we find much more detail.

The chapter starts, 'The Lord appeared to Abraham by the oaks of Mamre, as he sat at the entrance of his tent in the heat of the day.' We probably begin to wonder in what form the Lord appeared, and when we first heard the account we were almost certainly surprised as we went on to read, verse 2, 'He looked up and saw three men standing near him.' In verse 3 Abraham speaks to, 'My lord.' Clearly one of the three stands out as special. Later on in the account, at verse 22, we read, 'So the men turned from there, and went towards Sodom, while Abraham remained standing before the Lord.' And to complete the picture the first verse of the next chapter tells us that, 'The two angels came to Sodom.' So we have 'three men', one of whom seems to stand out and is addressed as, 'My lord.' Later two of them, who are now called angels, set off for Sodom, while Abraham remains standing before the third man, who is called, 'the Lord.' So here is an incident in which there is both the 'angel of the Lord', who seems to be either the Lord himself, or certainly acting with the full authority of the Lord, and also two other angelic beings.

This and the many other appearances that follow teach us

that there are angelic beings as well as God himself in what we call heaven. Heaven is not a place where God dwells in splendid isolation, but where he lives in community.

The third point that we ought to notice is that in some of the prophetic books, especially Isaiah, there are a number of descriptions of a state of perfection that will one day come, that can be taken as being just picturesque promises of a better future, or just possibly idealised pictures of the church in this present age, or both; but which at a deeper level suggest that there is also to come, something that cannot be completely fulfilled in this world as it now is, but only in a completely re-created world, or in some other order of things altogether, namely what we call heaven. We will refer back to these passages when we deal with some of the descriptions given in the New Testament which tie in with them.

This background from the Old Testament may seem to be thin, not fully formed, not clearly expressed, but it is nevertheless very important because any supposed teaching from the New Testament that does not have a foundation in the Old Testament is to be treated with suspicion.

Whilst not wanting to be too seriously diverted at this point, a summary of the Old Testament on this subject would be incomplete if we did not mention that there are also things in the books of Ezekiel and Daniel that some believe refer to things that come after the end of this world as it presently is. We will take a brief look at these things in the next two chapters, which we may like to look upon as signposts warning us of the two diversions we will encounter later in our journey.

5

Ezekiel

The last nine chapters of Ezekiel, chapters 40 – 48, contain a long and detailed description of a vision, or visions, of a restored land with a restored city and, at its heart, a restored temple. This vision was a message to the Israelites in captivity about what was to come in the future. The details are very precise, even down to the widths of individual gateways.

What we know for certain is that this city and this temple have never yet been built. The temple built when the people returned from captivity was nothing like this, and the temple built by Herod in the time of Jesus was nothing like this. This has led some to argue that it must still be in the future, and must in fact belong to a time after this world as it now is has come to an end.

It seems to me that there are insuperable difficulties to such an idea. For example it gives detailed rules for the sacrifices to be offered by the priests in this temple. If this temple belongs to the life to come, it destroys the teaching that the Old Testament sacrificial system was completed in, and superseded by, the death of Jesus Christ on the cross. The whole Christian era becomes a temporary phase after which we are back in an Old Testament system.

Perhaps even more devastating to this idea is the fact that in Ezekiel's vision the temple is absolutely central, whereas in the vision of the new Jerusalem in Revelation we read, Revelation 21:22 'I saw no temple in the city, for its temple is the Lord God the Almighty and the Lamb.'

For these, and many other reasons, most commentators agree that this is a highly developed illustration of the kind of society and its worship that God delights in. Read in this way it is not about something strange in the future, but about how godliness is to be shown in this life now. As such, it is full of inspiring teaching, and is relevant to all times.

6

Daniel

In a somewhat similar way, the last six chapters of Daniel, chapters 7 – 12, contain a number of visions that are a happy hunting ground for people who want to work out schemes and dates for the future. Some people find in these chapters things that they think refer to the life to come. Most scholars think this way of understanding them is mistaken and suggest that they refer symbolically to the rise and fall of earthly kingdoms in this life.

What is more certain is that we are on dangerous ground when we try to use them to establish things to do with the future for they include the words, Daniel 12:8–9, 'I heard but could not understand; so I said, "My lord, what shall be the outcome of these things?" He said, "Go your way, Daniel, for the words are to remain secret and sealed until the time of the end."'

It seems wisest to learn from these visions that God is in control, and so all will work out right in the end, and to leave the rest with God. It is not necessarily wrong to speculate about what empires the visions may refer to, but it is very dangerous to use such speculations as a basis for any doctrine.

The book finishes with the words, 'But you, go your

way, and rest; you shall rise for your reward at the end of the days' (Daniel 12:13). This comment, another of those tantalising pointers to something without actually saying what it is, enables us to leave this brief look at the Old Testament with our eyes refocused on the subject of heaven.

7

The Four Gospels

As we enter the Gospels we find a flurry of angelic activity. In Matthew we have the story from Joseph's viewpoint. We read of how he was puzzling over what to do about his young wife to be, whom he loved dearly but who was pregnant with a baby that definitely was not his, and then we read, Matthew 1:20, 'an angel of the Lord appeared to him in a dream and said, "Joseph, son of David, do not be afraid to take Mary as your wife, for the child conceived in her is from the Holy Spirit."' And 'the angel of the Lord' appears to him twice more in chapter 2 to help him in protecting and caring for the precious child.

In Luke, by contrast, we have the story from Mary's viewpoint. First we have a section about the birth of John the Baptist, with 'the angel of the Lord', appearing to Zechariah in Luke 1:11, and in verse 19 we get the interesting statement, 'I am Gabriel. I stand in the presence of God, and I have been sent to speak to you and bring you this good news.' Interesting because it shows that, in this case at least, the 'angel of the Lord' cannot be God himself, but is an angel acting on the authority of God.

Then in verse 26 we come to Mary's story, 'In the sixth month the angel Gabriel was sent by God to a town in

Galilee called Nazareth, to a virgin engaged to a man whose name was Joseph.'

And then in chapter 2 we have the remarkable experience of the shepherds. First we have in verses 8–12, 'an angel of the Lord' appearing to them, and then in verse 13 we read, 'And suddenly there was with the angel a multitude of the heavenly host, praising God and saying, "Glory to God in the highest heaven, and on earth peace among those whom he favours!"' Something so tremendous is taking place down here on earth, that all the heavenly host want to be involved, and so the whole choir come along! Seriously – here we see a contact point between 'the highest heaven' and earth. This shows us that heaven is not a place where there are just a few special angels, but that it is teeming with a host of angels who love to sing God's praises. It also indicates that 'the highest heaven' is not just a description of the outer atmosphere, or even of space, but is where God dwells. We are not yet given any description of it, but we are shown that it definitely exists.

In passing we may note that though Mark and John do not tell us about the birth of Jesus, they each bring angels into their accounts at an early stage, see Mark 1:13 and John 1:51.

This is not meant to be a book about angels, but they are important to our study, firstly because they help to show that heaven exists, and secondly because Jesus said that in the life to come the redeemed will be like the angels in heaven, and so what angels are like may give us clues as to what we will be like. We can note that angels may 'appear' and 'disappear', which may remind us of the resurrected Jesus Christ, but whilst they are on this earth they seem to be very solid and real – they eat food, they walk around, they talk, they can even wrestle with a man (Genesis

32:22–32), unless we take that passage to be about God himself. This again may remind us of the resurrected Jesus. In all of this it may be true that they are assuming a form that is suitable for meeting with people on this earth, but we should probably deduce from it that the heavenly state is not a vague ethereal thing, but something every bit as solid and real as this earthly life we now live. Hebrew thought could not really envisage any form of existence that did not have a body, and in this they were being true to their scriptures.

Is there any direct teaching about heaven given by Jesus? Well, yes, of course we know there is, for we all know the Lord's Prayer: Matthew 6:9–10, 'Our Father in heaven, hallowed be your name. Your kingdom come. Your will be done, on earth as it is in heaven.' So here is some very basic teaching: God is in heaven and it is a place where his will is done. No detail there, but it is fundamental, and there are several other times when Jesus describes God as the 'Father in heaven' or as the 'heavenly Father'.

We may, for convenience, divide the teaching of Jesus on this subject into three categories. First there are those parts in Matthew, Mark and Luke that clearly refer to something after this life here on earth. Secondly there is a mass of teaching on what Matthew calls 'the kingdom of heaven' and Mark and Luke call 'the kingdom of God'. Thirdly there is the extra teaching recorded by John. These will be the subject of the next three chapters.

8

Matthew, Mark and Luke

After all the excitement with angels at the birth of Jesus, the first pointer to the life to come actually comes from the lips of John the Baptist speaking about Jesus, Matthew 3:12, 'His winnowing-fork is in his hand, and he will clear his threshing-floor and will gather his wheat into the granary; but the chaff he will burn with unquenchable fire.' and similarly in Luke 3:17. Here is an agricultural illustration of something being done for a purpose – to lead to a harvest. After the weeds have been removed and destroyed, good seed will be gathered in. Being gathered into a granary may not sound very exciting, or attractive, but the point is that there is a purposeful future.

From an agricultural illustration we move on to a maritime illustration: Matthew 4:19, 'Follow me, and I will make you fish for people.' That doesn't tell us much, but it does again raise the question of, 'What for?' There is a purposeful future.

We will have more to say about the Beatitudes in the next chapter, but from it we can now notice, Matthew 5:12, 'Rejoice and be glad, for your reward is great in heaven.' and similarly in Luke 6:23. This begins to sound a bit more exciting, not just stored in a granary, but rewards to celebrate.

In Mark 9:43–49 and Matthew 18:8–9 Jesus says that it will be better to make great sacrifices and enter into 'life', than to act complacently and be lost, or worse. The point for our study is that the life to come is described by Jesus as 'life'. Any view of heaven which thinks of people there as being asleep or as automatons, or any such idea, is wrong. It is a place or state of 'life'.

This 'life' is mentioned again in Matthew 7:13–14, 'Enter through the narrow gate; for the gate is wide and the road is easy that leads to destruction, and there are many that take it. For the gate is narrow and the road is hard that leads to life, and there are few that find it.' And there is a similar passage in Luke 13:23–24.

An important piece of teaching comes in Matthew 6:19–21, 'Do not store up for yourselves treasures on earth, where moth and rust consume and where thieves break in and steal; but store up for yourselves treasures in heaven, where neither moth nor rust consumes and where thieves do not break in and steal. For where your treasure is, there your heart will be also.' And there is a similar passage in Luke 12:33–34 where it is specifically linked with the giving of alms.

We can glean at least three things about heaven from these passages. Firstly, what we do in this life has a connection with our situation in heaven, and this applies especially to our use of money – a message that also comes from Matthew 19:21 and its parallels in Mark and Luke. Secondly, heaven is a place of security. And thirdly, we need to take these things seriously, which is also part of the message of the previous quotation about the narrow gate.

Matthew 18:10 is another passage that emphasises a closer link between this life and heaven than we may sometimes think – 'Take care that you do not despise one of these little ones; for, I tell you, in heaven their angels continually see the face of my Father in heaven.' And this interlinking can also be seen in Matthew 18:18, 'Truly I tell you, whatever you bind on earth will be bound in heaven, and whatever you loose on earth will be loosed in heaven.'

In passing, it may be wise to mention that the story of the rich man and Lazarus in Luke 16:19–31 is not about what we call heaven and hell, but about Hades, the place of the departed before the judgment. Lazarus is in peace at Abraham's side, but he is not yet in heaven.

We find some more important teaching in Matthew 22:23–33 and the parallel passages in Mark and Luke. The Sadducees, who only accepted the first five books of the Bible and who did not believe in any form of life after death, come to Jesus with their ridiculous, but cunning, story of the woman who had been married successively to seven brothers, and so, they ask, Matthew 22:28, 'In the resurrection, then, whose wife of the seven will she be? For all of them had married her.' Jesus is going to go on to show the Sadducees that the fact of coming resurrection can be shown from those few books of the Bible they did accept; but before that he says, Matthew 22:29–30, 'You are wrong, because you know neither the scriptures nor the power of God. For in the resurrection they neither marry nor are given in marriage, but are like angels in heaven.'

We can find several things from that reply. Firstly, if we know the Scriptures properly we will believe in heaven. Secondly, if we think the idea of heaven is impossible then we have not understood the power of God. Thirdly, the life of heaven is not to be thought of as just a simple continuation of this life on earth, there is a difference – we will be like angels. Fourthly, the word heaven at the end could be simply a description of the angels, but equally it could be saying that the redeemed will be in heaven along with the angels. And fifthly, what angels are like will tell us something about what we will be like, which partly explains our earlier interest in angels.

Matthew 24 and parallel passages tell us about the destruction of Jerusalem and the end of the age. Whilst strictly speaking not relating to the topic of heaven, these things feature prominently in some of the many different ideas about the 'end times'. Verses 30–31 tell us that the day will come when 'the Son of Man' (Jesus) will come again, and his 'elect' will be gathered together, but it does not tell us where they will be gathered to, or taken to; for that we have to wait until 1 Thessalonians.

At the Last Supper, Jesus said, Matthew 26:29, 'I will never again drink of this fruit of the vine until that day when I drink it new with you in my Father's kingdom.' This statement can lead us into the whole subject of Christ's teaching related to eating, drinking and feasting. Banquets and wedding feasts were regular features of his parables, and when he gave a special way by which he was to be remembered, it was by means of a meal. With Jesus at its centre it is hard not to imagine that there will be a considerable amount of celebrating in heaven.

Thinking of wedding feasts, there is no teaching given by Jesus that actually said that he would be married to his people, but he came very close to it. That, and the Old Testament background of verses like Isaiah 54:5, 'For your Maker is your husband.' (See also Isaiah 62:4 and Hosea 2:19), was to lead to important teaching in the Epistles and to a great illustration in Revelation.

9

The Kingdom of Heaven

In the Gospels there are many references by Jesus to the kingdom of heaven, generally in parables, but also in other contexts. We will look at them in a separate chapter because they need to be seen in a slightly different way to other references about heaven. To begin with we need to be aware that, Matthew's references to the kingdom of heaven, are by Mark and Luke rendered as kingdom of God. So we cannot simply say they are about heaven.

Perhaps the easiest way to understand them comes from concentrating on the word, kingdom, and to link this with the words in the Lord's Prayer, 'Your kingdom come. Your will be done, on earth as it is in heaven.' These passages are about God's rule, whether it be in heaven or on earth, they are therefore just as much about things down here on earth as they are to do with heaven. However, because the Lord's Prayer says that God's kingdom has come, and his will is done, in heaven, then any teaching about how God's kingdom is to come on earth will give us some degree of understanding of what already exists in heaven.

The first two references are identical words spoken by both John the Baptist in Matthew 3:2 and by Jesus in Matthew 4:17, 'Repent, for the kingdom of heaven has come near.' That both John, the forerunner; and Jesus, the one for whom he prepared the way; said the same thing, indicates strongly that this kingdom is intricately connected with Jesus. Through Jesus we will hear of it, through him we will enter it, and in it we will find him. We will learn more about this connection when we consider John's Gospel in the next chapter.

In Luke 4:43 Jesus says, 'I must proclaim the good news of the kingdom of God.' This doesn't tell us what it is, except that it is good news. And in Matthew 4:23 we read, 'Jesus went throughout Galilee, teaching in their synagogues and proclaiming the good news of the kingdom and curing every disease and every sickness among the people.' This suggests to us that at least one aspect of this good news is to do with healing and wholeness; and this is an important part of one of the pictures in Revelation.

Next we come to the Beatitudes, which start with, Matthew 5:3, 'Blessed are the poor in spirit, for theirs is the kingdom of heaven.' We may link this with Isaiah 57:15, 'For thus says the high and lofty one who inhabits eternity, whose name is Holy: I dwell in the high and holy place, and also with those who are contrite and humble in spirit.' Or, as *The Living Bible* paraphrase rather beautifully puts it, 'I live in that high and holy place where those with contrite, humble spirits dwell.' We must not push this too far, but we can surely glean that the kingdom of heaven, and heaven itself, is characterised by humility. (See also Matthew 18:1–5)

At the other end of the Beatitudes we have, Matthew 5:10, 'Blessed are those who are persecuted for righteousness' sake, for theirs is the kingdom of heaven.' The implication of having this reference to the kingdom of heaven at both the start and the end of the Beatitudes is that even if it is not mentioned by name in the others, it is actually the unwritten subject of all of them; and so we can deduce that the characteristics of the kingdom of heaven, and so also of heaven itself, are all the things mentioned in verses 3–10, things like: humility, meekness, a hunger for righteousness, mercy, purity and peace.

Shortly after this Jesus says in Matthew 5:19, 'whoever breaks one of the least of these commandments, and teaches others to do the same, will be called least in the kingdom of heaven; but whoever does them and teaches them will be called great in the kingdom of heaven.' We will not get tied up in a discussion about what command-ments these are, but simply notice that Jesus seems to be teaching that there will be different levels in heaven – some called least and some great. We may well have an idea of a place of absolute equality, but this would point to a differ-ent understanding. This is an idea that fits in well with there being archangels as well as angels.

Matthew 7:21, 'Not everyone who says to me, "Lord, Lord", will enter the kingdom of heaven, but only one who does the will of my Father in heaven.' This is not a matter of words, but of the right spirit showing itself in deeds.

In Matthew 11:12 we have some notoriously difficult words from the lips of Jesus, 'From the days of John the Baptist until now the kingdom of heaven has suffered vio-lence, and the violent take it by force.' None of the possible variant translations are in practice any easier. Perhaps the best thing we can do with this verse is to learn humility and admit that there are some things we don't understand. I have my own particular ideas but all I would say here is that it centres on the ministry of Jesus, for that was the period of time 'from the days of John the Baptist until now.'

And now we come to a number of parables of the

kingdom – parables that generally start with the words, 'The kingdom of heaven [or God] is like . . .', though there are minor variations. In that Jesus said to his disciples, John 16:33, 'In the world you face persecution. But take courage; I have conquered the world!' and yet some of these parables look forward to something wonderful to come; we can safely say that while they may be about the kingdom of heaven coming on earth, some of them at least must also look forward to the perfection that will only be attained in heaven itself, and so can be seen as revealing something about the nature of heaven. Here, in brief, are those that could be seen to be in this category.

The Parable of the Weeds – Matthew 13:24–30 – which teaches us that only the 'wheat' will end up in God's barn. Not everyone will be there.

The Parable of the Mustard Seed – Matthew 13:31–32 (also Mark and Luke) – which could be taken to point to heaven being unexpectedly large, i.e. beyond our comprehension.

The Hidden Treasure – Matthew 13:44 – stumbled upon seemingly by accident and found to be worth everything.

The Pearl – Matthew 13:45–46 – sought for until found and then considered to be worth everything.

The Net – Matthew 13:47–50 – which again teaches that not everyone will get there.

The Unmerciful Servant – Matthew 18:23–35 – which teaches us that no one can be there without forgiveness.

The Marriage Feast – Matthew 22:1–14 (also Luke) – which teaches that all kinds of people are invited, but that they must come properly dressed. This can be taken to mean that while everyone may come, they cannot come in their own right, they can only come wearing the righteousness of Christ. Some commentators think the part at the end about the wedding robe ought not to be there, I suggest that it very much ought to be there, it is an integral part of the teaching. Jesus is not saying that anyone can come, but that anyone can come as long as they come by the right way.

So, here we have clear teaching that there is such a place as heaven; that it is significantly different from life on this earth; that it is a place, or state, of perfection; that it is for those who are humble, for those who have been forgiven and have shown their forgiveness by forgiving others, those who come with their sins taken away and wearing instead the righteousness of Christ. (That last bit comes more clearly from the Epistles which we will look at later.) All of this is very important, but we may feel that it doesn't tell us very much about what heaven will actually be like. Has John got more to tell us?

10

The Gospel of John

Matthew, Mark and Luke have been concerned to tell us the facts about the ministry of Jesus. John is also concerned about facts and goes out of his way to tell us that what he has recorded is the truth, but his approach is more that of a sermon. His purpose is not just to convey facts, but to bring his readers to a conviction, the conviction clearly stated in, John 20:31, 'But these are written so that you may come to believe that Jesus is the Messiah, the Son of God, and that through believing you may have life in his name.' And so we tend to find more in it that points to the meaning of it all; it could almost be seen as being half way between the facts of Matthew, Mark and Luke; and the teaching of the Epistles. We may therefore expect to find that what John records that relates to heaven is more explicit about its nature.

In describing the call of Nathaniel, John records Jesus as saying to him, John 1:51, 'Very truly, I tell you, you will see heaven opened and the angels of God ascending and descending upon the Son of Man.' As we read through the story it becomes apparent that Nathaniel has been meditating on the story of Jacob's ladder with the angels ascending and descending on it. Jesus somehow knows what he has been thinking and applies the story to himself. In effect he is saying, 'As Jacob in his dream saw a link between heaven and earth, so you will come to see that link in me.' Here is a forerunner of something he was going to say more openly later – 'I am the way.' He is the way to heaven.

In his conversation with Nicodemus, John 3, Jesus makes it clear that to see and enter the kingdom of God you must be born from above, born of the spirit, born again. This needs to be held in balance with other passages that speak of being adopted into God's family. Jesus is saying that to be in God's family, to belong to heaven, you must be made part of that family. It doesn't just happen automatically, it is a very definite transaction that has to take place. In verses 14–16 he goes on to refer to the time when the Israelites in the wilderness were being bitten by poisonous snakes. God told Moses to erect a pole with a model of a snake on it, and the people were told that anyone who looked at it would be healed from their bite. Those that did not look were not healed, it was a very definite transaction. Jesus then says that he is going to be lifted up so that those who believe in him may have eternal life. He is the way from death to life, he is the way to eternal life, to heaven. The final verse of chapter 3 is very definite, 'Whoever believes in the Son has eternal life; whoever disobeys the Son will not see life, but must endure God's wrath.' Jesus is being presented as not only 'the way' but also as 'the door' about which we will also hear more later.

We may have noticed already that, as recorded by John, Christ's favourite way of speaking of life after death is simply as, 'life', or sometimes as, 'eternal life'. And so for example we have John 5:24, 'Very truly, I tell you, anyone who hears my word and believes him that sent me has eternal life, and does not come under judgment, but has passed from death to life.'

In chapter 10, talking about the good shepherd, Jesus says, John 10:9, 'I am the gate. Whoever enters by me will be saved.' And 10:10, 'I came that they may have life, and have it abundantly.'

And so we move on to John 14:1–6,

'Do not let your hearts be troubled. Believe in God, believe also in me. In my Father's house there are many dwelling places. If it were not so, would I have told you that I go to prepare a place for you? And if I go and prepare a place for you, I will come again and take you to myself, so that where I am, there you may be also. And you know the way to the place where I am going.' Thomas said to him, 'Lord, we do not know where you are going. How can we know the way?' Jesus said to him, 'I am the way, and the truth, and the life. No one comes to the Father except through me.'

First we can notice, what we have already seen, that Jesus is adamant that he is 'the way', and he is so completely the way to life, that he is also 'the life'.

Secondly we can take a closer look at this description of heaven, as 'my Father's house'. It is a natural enough description of heaven, one of the primary definitions of which is that it is, where God dwells. What is new here is that in it there are 'dwelling places' which Jesus will prepare for his followers. What does this mean?

Generations of Christians who were brought up on the King James Version with its translation of, 'In my Father's house are many mansions.' and living at a time when a mansion meant a large house; have been misled into thinking of rows of attractive big houses, in which each Christian would live in 'splendid isolation'. However when that translation was first made, a mansion more normally meant separate rooms in a larger building; and the original Greek word comes from a root meaning 'to stay', and itself simply means 'a place to stay'. It can be a room, it can be a large building, but when put into the context of, 'in my Father's house' it clearly means a room, or rooms. At first sight this may seem disappointing to people whose concept of heaven included the house of their dreams, just for them. But all disappointment ought to vanish when we understand what it is really about. It is about children of the King, living in the palace, with a full right to roam throughout the whole palace, but within it also having their own private quarters. Jesus words could be thought of as being something like when we are planning to visit friends, and they say, 'We will make up a bed for you.' We don't expect that bed to be in a shed at the bottom of the garden, nor do we expect to be confined to that one room. We are being invited into their home, but within it we will have our own room.

A few years ago my wife and I went to stay with a friend in America. She had recently moved into a new split-level house. The main living quarters were on one level, and below it was a separate suite of rooms for guests. We had complete control of two bedrooms, a bathroom and a large sitting room; in our friend's house was our own special dwelling place; but we also had complete freedom to be anywhere, and to use anything, on the main floor. We lived in our friend's house, but within it we also had our own resting place.

This can be taken to teach that in heaven we will be fully part of God's family with all the rights that go with such a position, and yet we will still retain our individuality.

Again we see the very close link between heaven and Jesus. It is his Father's house, and he is going to prepare the place for us there. We don't have to worry about how we will find our way around in heaven, Jesus will meet us, show us everything we need to know, and show us our own special place within it. He is the way, both to it and also within it. And we don't have to worry about whether there will be room for us – there are plenty of rooms.

We will look later (in Chapter 22) at the exclusive nature of the words, 'No one comes to the Father except through me.'

We find some important points in Christ's great prayer in John 17. In verse 16 he says of his disciples, 'They do not belong to the world, just as I do not belong to the world.' He has already said, verse 5, 'So now, Father, glorify me in your presence with the glory that I had in your presence before the world existed.' And he goes on to say in verse 24, 'Father, I desire that those also, whom you have given me, may be with me where I am, to see my glory, which you have given me because you loved me before the foundation of the world.'

Another point, that may seem obvious, but which is also obviously very important, that comes from this prayer, and other parts of John's Gospel, is the centrality of love in heaven.

There is much more that could be drawn out of the four Gospels than has been presented in these last four chapters, for example this might be the logical place to look at what we can learn from the nature of the resurrection body of Jesus, but I have found it easier to be able to refer back to the teaching in the Epistles when dealing with this subject so we will look at it in chapter 17 after going through the Epistles.

11

The Teaching of Acts

The book of Acts is all about what God is doing by his Spirit in the early church, and it is therefore not surprising that we do not find much about heaven.

In chapter 20 Paul meets with the elders of the church in Ephesus before saying his final farewell to them. Towards the end he says, verse 32, 'And now I commend you to God and to the message of his grace, a message that is able to build you up and to give you the inheritance among all who are sanctified.' An inheritance is something that is inherited. Paul is speaking of the future that is theirs because they are the children of God. Heaven is not something we can get into because we have earned it, or are worth it, but something we inherit because we are children.

Peter speaking in Acts 3:20–21 says, 'so that times of refreshing may come from the presence of the Lord, and that he may send the Messiah appointed for you, that is, Jesus, who must remain in heaven until the time of universal restoration that God announced long ago through his holy prophets.'

What is this about? What is this 'time of universal restoration'? Some argue that all the prophetic visions of a time of perfection will be literally fulfilled in a restored world, over which Jesus will come to reign in person, but there are other legitimate alternative understandings. This is the first of four New Testament passages that together with Isaiah 65:17–25 seem, at first sight, to differ from the other Bible teaching and say that our future is to be thought of as being on this earth. Taken in the wrong way we can easily create a conflict between two opposing views and we may think that we have to accept either the one or the other, but it is perfectly possible to find an enriching reconciliation that brings all the teaching together. However working this out needs careful thought so these passages – Isaiah 65:17–25 and Acts 3:19–21 – will be the first two of five passages that we will study in our second diversion in chapter 21.

12

The Teaching of Paul

The first reference in Romans that may be relevant is in Romans 2:7, 'to those who by patiently doing good seek for glory and honour and immortality, he will give eternal life.' And he goes on to say, in Romans 2:10, that this will mean, 'glory and honour and peace for everyone who does good, the Jew first and also the Greek.' We notice that the scope of this is universal – all, of any race, may be included, as long as they come on the right basis. But we may also take note that Paul is going to go on to show that in practice no one is justified by their own good deeds and that therefore to enter into this blessing they will need the righteousness of Christ, which we have previously identified as the wedding garment in the Gospel parable. (See also Romans 3:23–24).

In Romans 5:1–2 Paul sums up what as Christians we have now, and what we hope for in the future. 'Therefore, since we are justified by faith, we have peace with God through our Lord Jesus Christ, through whom we have obtained access to this grace in which we stand; and we boast in our hope of sharing the glory of God.' That seems to me to be a pretty bold and glorious hope, tying in closely with Christ's prayer for his disciples and with his promise of going to be with him in his Father's house.

This is expressed more fully in Romans 6:5–8,

> For if we have been united with him in a death like his, we will
> certainly be united with him in a resurrection like his. We
> know that our old self was crucified with him so that the body
> of sin might be destroyed, and we might no longer be enslaved
> to sin. For whoever has died is freed from sin. But if we have
> died with Christ, we believe that we will also live with him.

Here we see that the whole matter is centred on Christ and
ends with us being with him.

And now we come to Romans 8:19–23,

> For the creation waits with eager longing for the revealing of
> the children of God; for the creation was subjected to futility,
> not of its own will but by the will of the one who subjected it,
> in hope that the creation itself will be set free from its bondage
> to decay and will obtain the freedom of the glory of the chil-
> dren of God. We know that the whole creation has been
> groaning in labour pains until now; and not only the creation,
> but we ourselves, who have the first fruits of the Spirit, groan
> inwardly while we wait for adoption, the redemption of our
> bodies.

This is a very complex passage about which some commentators have written a great many pages; it is the third
of the five passages we will look at in chapter 21.

After three chapters on the place of Israel in the continu-
ing plans of God, Paul moves into practical instructions for
living the Christian life, and so we can find nothing more
relevant to the topic of heaven, unless we treat it like we
treated the Gospel passages about the kingdom of heaven
and see, in the way Christians are to behave, a reflection of
what heaven is like.

In 1 Corinthians 3:16–17 we come to a statement which may not, at first sight, seem to have anything to do with heaven, but which we may later find to be very relevant, 'Do you not know that you are God's temple and that God's Spirit dwells in you? If anyone destroys God's temple, God will destroy that person. For God's temple is holy, and you are that temple.' (See also 1 Corinthians 6:19–20)

In the great chapter 13 we are told that three things will carry on into the life to come: faith, hope, and most important of all, love. We may well follow Christopher Wordsworth's well-known hymn in thinking that, 'Faith will vanish into sight; hope be emptied in delight;' but the relationship with God that they express can be expected to continue and is impossible to disentangle from love.

Most of 1 Corinthians is answering a series of special questions which do not relate to our topic, but the great chapter on resurrection, chapter 15, needs careful attention. Firstly it states very clearly that if there is no resurrection then Christ was not raised, and if Christ was not raised then our faith is futile. The whole chapter ought to be read, but in particular Paul deals with the nature of the resurrection body in 1 Corinthians 15:42–44, 'What is sown is perishable, what is raised is imperishable. It is sown in dishonour, it is raised in glory. It is sown in weakness, it is raised in power. It is sown a physical body, it is raised a spiritual body.' This is very clear. This future body differs in some way from our present body for it is to be suitable for a spiritual existence rather than this present physical existence. However if we look on to verses 50–54 we find that there is still a very close link with this present body – 1 Corinthians 15:52–53, 'For the trumpet will sound, and the dead will be raised imperishable, and we will be changed. For this perishable body must put on imperishability, and this mortal body must put on immortality.' Perhaps this is best described as change with continuity. Here is teaching that we may well think should also have some bearing on how we think of the relationship of heaven to the earth on which we now live. Will the links between the 'two bodies' in which we live also apply to the 'two places' where we live?

In 1 Corinthians 15:23–24, Paul says of the resurrection, 'But each in his own order: Christ the first fruits, then at his coming those who belong to Christ. Then comes the end, when he hands over the kingdom to God the Father.' The first two steps are straightforward, Christ was raised about 2000 years ago, we will be raised when Christ comes again; but there is a disagreement about the words, 'Then comes the end.' Some see this as simply stating that this is the end of the history of the earth. Others think that it implies an interval after the second coming before 'the end', and this can be linked up with ideas about the 'thousand years' mentioned in Revelation 20. We will endeavour to reach a conclusion on this later.

In 2 Corinthians we come to an important section in 5:1–5,

> For we know that if the earthly tent we live in is destroyed, we have a building from God, a house not made with hands, eternal in the heavens. For in this tent we groan, longing to be clothed with our heavenly dwelling – if indeed, when we have taken it off we will not be found naked. For while we are still in this tent, we groan under our burden, because we wish not to be unclothed but to be further clothed, so that what is mortal may be swallowed up in life. He who has prepared us for this very thing is God, who has given us the Spirit as a guarantee.

Here Paul is not talking about dwelling places in God's house, but using buildings to illustrate the difference between our earthly body and the spiritual body. He likens this earthly body to a tent, a temporary, passing thing; by contrast the heavenly body is likened to a substantial and permanent house; and where is this house? It is in the heavens. What is made very clear is that we are not to think of a future existence as disembodied spirits, but as having a very definite body. Not less real than this earthly body, but far more real. Paul seems to look on being disembodied as being almost impossible. Those who go to heaven will have a very real body, not earthly, but heavenly and far more lasting than this earthly body in which 'we groan'.

Galatians is taken up with correcting things that have gone wrong and nothing can be found relating to heaven, except perhaps a short reference to 'harvest time' in Galatians 6:9.

By contrast Ephesians, which was probably in origin a 'round robin' letter to be circulated to several churches, is not dealing with a few special problems, but is a carefully prepared treatise on basic doctrine. We would expect to find something here about the life to come. We will not be disappointed.

Ephesians 1:3, 'Blessed be the God and Father of our Lord Jesus Christ, who has blessed us in Christ with every spiritual blessing in the heavenly places.' Right at the start Paul is pointing his readers up beyond this present world, to the heavenly places; and at the end of that first paragraph he says, 1:13–14, 'In him you also, when you had heard the word of truth, the gospel of your salvation, and had believed in him, were marked with the seal of the promised Holy Spirit; this is the pledge of our inheritance towards redemption as God's own people, to the praise of his glory.' Here Paul is saying that the gift of the Spirit in this life is a pledge that we will one day enter into the fullness of our inheritance as God's own people; something we have come across already in 2 Corinthians 5:5. And a few verses later he is praying, 1:17–18,

> I pray that the God of our Lord Jesus Christ, the Father of glory, may give you a spirit of wisdom and revelation as you come to know him, so that, with the eyes of your heart enlightened, you may know what is the hope to which he has called you, what are the riches of his glorious inheritance among the saints.

A further hint of what this means comes in 2:6–7, 'and raised us up with him and seated us with him in the heavenly places with Christ Jesus, so that in the ages to come he might show the immeasurable riches of his grace in kindness towards us in Christ Jesus.' Our minds may well boggle at what exactly this all means, but we will surely be encouraged by that word, 'kindness'. We are not going to be overwhelmed by something we cannot cope with, we will be blessed kindly.

At the end of the second chapter Paul uses another building illustration, 2:19–22,

> So then you are no longer strangers and aliens, but you are citizens with the saints and also members of the household of God, built upon the foundation of the apostles and prophets, with Christ Jesus himself as the cornerstone. In him the whole structure is joined together and grows into a holy temple in the Lord; in whom you are built together spiritually into a dwelling place for God.

We may take this as a picture of the church on earth, which we have already seen is to be the temple of God, but in the context of these first two chapters it seems to also point ahead to an even greater fulfilment in the life to come, and will fit in closely with some things in the book of Revelation.

In chapter 5 Paul deals with relationships and in speaking of marriage he gets carried away and uses marriage as an illustration of the relationship between Christ and the church. 5:31–32, '"For this reason a man will leave his father and mother and be joined to his wife, and the two will become one flesh." This is a great mystery, and I am applying it to Christ and the church.' This also will tie up closely with some things in the book of Revelation.

In Philippians we have a lovely personal declaration by Paul in 1:21–24,

> For to me, living is Christ and dying is gain. If I am to live in the flesh, that means fruitful labour for me; and I do not know which I prefer. I am hard pressed between the two: my desire is to depart and be with Christ, for that is far better; but to remain in the flesh is more necessary for you.

Paul concludes that God wants him to labour on a bit longer. For our study the important point is that Paul speaks as though at death he will go directly to be with Christ. This is a lovely and comforting thought, but it raises some questions. What has happened to the general resurrection and the Day of Judgment? In other places those who have died are described as 'sleeping', they are not thought of as being already in heaven, but are in Hades, the place, or state, of waiting for the final judgment, so how can we square this with Paul's apparent assertion that he would go to be with Christ immediately?

Firstly we need to note that Paul does not necessarily

mean this, he could be meaning that the next thing he will know is that he will be with Christ. He is on this earth. He dies (falls asleep). He wakes up and finds he is with Christ. Some such thoughts may run parallel with the fact that we have no idea what time means in the life to come. We may also note that in some manuscripts in 1 Thessalonians 4:14 Christians who have died are described as 'those who sleep in Jesus'; and this can be linked with Christ's parable of the rich man and Lazarus in Luke 16, which is about Hades, the place, or state, after death, but before the judgment; and its description of Lazarus as being with Abraham. In other words, while he waits, he is with the best possible company; for the Christian the best possible company would be Christ. We may imagine a Christian dying, and peacefully sleeping 'in Christ' until the great day when he rises up in his new spiritual body to be with Christ for ever. This book is meant to be about what is revealed in the Bible, but this is probably one of the points where we can only imagine, for the meaning of 'time' after death is beyond our comprehension.

And in Philippians 3:20–21 he says,

> But our citizenship is in heaven, and it is from there that we are expecting a Saviour, the Lord Jesus Christ. He will transform the body of our humiliation so that it may be conformed to the body of his glory, by the power which enables him to make all things subject to himself.

We have heard before of the two bodies: the physical and the spiritual, the tent and the house; here it is reinforced that they are not two entirely separate bodies, but one transformed into the other, in other words there will be a link between the two, there will be change with continuity.

I would suggest that at the very least this means that we will retain our individuality and in some way be recognisable.

Paul starts his letter to the Colossians as follows: Colossians 1:3–5,

> In our prayers for you we always thank God, the Father of our Lord Jesus Christ, for we have heard of your faith in Christ Jesus and of the love that you have for all the saints, because of the hope laid up for you in heaven. You have heard of this hope before in the word of truth, the gospel that has come to you.

The hope of heaven is the motivation for all that they do on earth. It was not a matter of 'being so heavenly minded that they were no earthly use.' as is rather unkindly said of some Christians. Rather it was a matter of being so heavenly minded that they were of great earthly use.

In 1:27 Paul declares to them the great mystery which has now been revealed, 'which is Christ in you, the hope of glory.' He is in them now by his Spirit, and he will be in them then.

Paul has a rousing message for them, and for us all, in 3:1–4,

> So if you have been raised with Christ, seek the things that are above, where Christ is, seated at the right hand of God. Set your mind on things that are above, not on things that are on earth, for you have died, and your life is hidden with Christ in God. When Christ who is your life is revealed, then you also will be revealed with him in glory.

Perhaps it is this Epistle above all others that urges us to think about what lies ahead of us in heaven, and to seek it diligently.

One of the main themes of both Paul's letters to the Thessalonians are questions about when Christ is going to come again, what will happen to those who have already died when that time comes, and what will happen to those who are still alive. Regarding those who are not redeemed, 2 Thessalonians 1:9 tells us that they will suffer eternal destruction, for a study of this I would refer you to my first book, *All You Need to Know About Hell*; but what about the redeemed? Let's look at 1 Thessalonians 4:13–18,

> But we do not want you to be uninformed, brothers and sisters, about those who have died, so that you may not grieve as others do who have no hope. For since we believe that Jesus died and rose again, even so, through Jesus, God will bring with him those who have died. For this we declare to you by the word of the Lord, that we who are alive, who are left until the coming of the Lord, will by no means precede those who have died. For the Lord himself, with a cry of command, with the archangel's call and with the sound of God's trumpet, will descend from heaven, and the dead in Christ will rise first. Then we who are alive, who are left, will be caught up in the clouds together with them to meet the Lord in the air; and so we will be with the Lord for ever. Therefore encourage one another with these words.

It may well be true that Paul expected this to happen in his lifetime, but Jesus had made it clear that no one apart from God knows when it will be, and the teaching is the same whether it happened in Paul's time, or whether it does not happen for another few thousand years.

We are told that the dead in Christ will rise first, that those living in Christ will then join them, and together we will all meet the Lord, and then we will all be with the Lord for ever. At its minimum this tells us that all in Christ, dead or alive, will meet the Lord and be with him for ever. What exactly is meant by the details of 'in the air' (a different word from that translated as heaven) and 'in the clouds' is really of little importance, except that it is definitely not on this earth.

Paul's letters to Timothy and Titus are mainly about the practical running of the church here on earth, but there are a surprising number of references to heaven.

1 Timothy 4:8, 'physical training is of some value, godliness is valuable in every way, holding promise for both the present life and the life to come.' That doesn't tell us anything about the life to come, but it does say that it exists, and we may find in it another hint to the continuity that we have come across before.

1 Timothy 6:18–19, 'They are to do good, to be rich in good works, generous, and ready to share, thus storing up for themselves the treasure of a good foundation for the future, so that they may take hold of the life that really is life.' It is most natural to understand that Paul is here speaking of the life of heaven, and that this is an echo of Jesus words in Matthew 6:20.

2 Timothy 4:8, 'From now on there is reserved for me the crown of righteousness, which the Lord, the righteous judge, will give to me on that day, and not only to me but also to all who have longed for his appearing.' And, 2 Timothy 4:18, 'The Lord will rescue me from every evil attack and save me for his heavenly kingdom. To him be the glory for ever and ever. Amen.' Paul is very clear about the reality of the heavenly kingdom and of the glories connected with it.

Titus 1:2, 'in the hope of eternal life that God, who never

lies, promised before the ages began.' 2:12–13, 'training us to renounce impiety and worldly passions, and in the present age to live lives that are self-controlled, upright, and godly, while we wait for the blessed hope and the manifestation of the glory of our great God and Saviour, Jesus Christ.' Paul shows us clearly that he considers the life to come to be of much more value than anything we can experience in this life on earth.

Finally we even find a snippet in the little letter to Philemon. Philemon had lost his runaway slave for a time, but he is now returning as a fellow Christian, and Paul says, verse 15, 'Perhaps this is the reason he was separated from you for a while, so that you might have him back for ever.' The relationship of master and slave was a short term, temporal thing. The relationship of being fellow children of God is something that will last for ever.

13

The Teaching of Hebrews and James

The letter to the Hebrews starts with magnificent words about Jesus Christ and tells us in verse 3 that he has 'sat down at the right hand of the Majesty on high', and in verse 4 that he is much more superior than the angels. In 2:10 we are told that in 'bringing many children to glory' Jesus is the 'pioneer'. So from the outset we are shown Jesus as the link-man in heaven and we might be expecting some great teaching on the subject, but in actual fact we are kept waiting in anticipation for some time as it hovers on the edge of saying things about heaven, without actually doing so. We may be left not entirely sure whether the 'rest', frequently referred to in chapters 3 – 4, is about this life or that to come, but by the end it becomes clearer.

In 5:9 Jesus is called, 'the source of eternal salvation', and this leads us on to 6:19-20, 'We have this hope, a sure and steadfast anchor, a hope that enters the inner shrine behind the curtain, where Jesus, a forerunner on our behalf, has entered, having become a priest for ever according to the order of Melchizedek.' Melchizedek was a priest who seemingly came from nowhere, with no ancestry to validate his right to be a priest, and yet he clearly was. In a similar way Jesus, humanly speaking came from the tribe of Judah, which was not the tribe from which priests came, yet he clearly is our great high priest (according to the order of Melchizedek). This is a legal point that is of importance to Jews, but may seem largely irrelevant to Gentiles. However the point that matters to all is that this high priest, Jesus, has entered into the Holy of holies, and has done so as our forerunner. We are to follow him there. He had won the right for us to be there, and he has secured the way for our entry, the rope that binds us to him is securely anchored there by himself. His presence there guarantees our eventual arrival. The earthly Holy of holies was a representation on earth of God's dwelling place in heaven. Jesus has entered the real Holy of holies in heaven, God's dwelling place, and that, amazingly, is our destination. It all fits in with Christ's words about, 'In my Father's house . . .' (John 14:1–6). And it will become an important part of another of the illustrations in the book of Revelation.

11:9–10, 'By faith he [Abraham] stayed for a time in the land he had been promised, as in a foreign land, living in tents, as did Isaac and Jacob, who were heirs with him of the same promise. For he looked forward to the city that has foundations, whose architect and builder is God.' Here we have a very close parallel with Paul's 'tent' and 'house' in 2 Corinthians 5:1–5.

11:15–16, 'If they had been thinking of the land they had left behind, they would have had opportunity to return. But as it is, they desire a better country, that is, a heavenly one. Therefore God is not ashamed to be called their God; indeed, he has prepared a city for them.'

The writer is saying that all the heroes of faith in this chapter 11 were living for a future promise, the promise of something better in the life to come. They never received it in this life. (*See* 11:39) And nor will we – 13:14, 'For here we have no lasting city, but we are looking for the city that is to come.' This was something that was seen, and still is to be seen, as being as much more substantial and desirable, as a city is more substantial and desirable than a tent; but we need to notice that it is a heavenly city, not an earthly one. In these passages we find ideas that will feed into another of the great illustrations in the book of Revelation.

James is written in the style of Hebrew wisdom literature, like the Old Testament book of Proverbs, and it is therefore not surprising that there is not much about heaven, but we can still find something hidden away in 1:12, 'Blessed is anyone who endures temptation. Such a one has stood the test and will receive the crown of life that the Lord has promised to those that love him.'

14

The Teaching of Peter

Peter begins his first letter with a wonderful doxology, the first part of which is as follows, 1 Peter 1:3–5,

> Blessed be the God and Father of our Lord Jesus Christ! By his great mercy he has given us a new birth into a living hope through the resurrection of Jesus Christ from the dead, and into an inheritance that is imperishable, undefiled, and unfading, kept in heaven for you, who are being protected by the power of God through faith for a salvation ready to be revealed in the last time.

What a marvellous outpouring. What a vision of heaven. 'Imperishable' and 'unfading' – this will fit in with the illustration of a city made of gold. 'Undefiled' – we will find many details to illustrate this in other pictures. And what a lovely thought, that a place is being kept for us who are being kept for it – another tie up with John 14:1–6, '. . . I go to prepare a place for you . . .'

Parts of chapter 2 are about being built into a spiritual house. This could be taken to be about the church here on earth, or about heaven. There is no reason why we should not apply it to both.

3:22 tells us in the clearest way what is the position of Jesus Christ in heaven, 'who has gone into heaven and is at the right hand of God, with angels, authorities, and powers made subject to him.'

We will look at 2 Peter together with Jude, as these two books have many similarities.

15

The Teaching of John

In his first letter, John says

> Do not love the world or the things in the world. The love of
> the Father is not in those who love the world; for all that is in
> the world – the desire of the flesh, the desire of the eyes, the
> pride in riches – comes not from the Father but from the world.
> And the world and its desires are passing away, but those who
> do the will of God live for ever. (1 John 2:15–17)

So this world is passing away, but the children of God will
not pass away with it, but will live for ever, somewhere. We
would like to know more clearly what exactly John sees the
nature of this somewhere to be, but he very honestly says,
3:2, 'Beloved, we are God's children now; what we will be
has not yet been revealed. What we do know is this: when
he is revealed, we will be like him, for we will see him as
he is.' So John says that we do not know all the answers,
but what he does say we know, is tremendous – we will be
like Jesus. No wonder John hesitates to take this any
further, the mind boggles at the possible implications.

In the rest of 1 John there is nothing directly about
heaven, but John does underline the relationship that is the

foundation for everything of lasting value, namely, that we love God and one another, and that God loves us.

The other two letters add nothing more.

16

The Teaching of 2 Peter and Jude

There is a staggering promise in 2 Peter 1:4, 'Thus he has given us, through these things, his precious and very great promises, so that through them you may escape from the corruption that is in the world because of lust, and may become participants in the divine nature.' We could take this to mean no more than that we will become a bit more like God, but it is more likely that it is pointing ahead to something much greater than that, something that we have just seen in 1 John 3:2.

In 3:7 Peter explains the final fate of this present world, 'But by the same word the present heavens and earth have been reserved for fire, being kept until the day of judgement and destruction of the godless.' And he elaborates further in 3:10, 'But the day of the Lord will come like a thief, and then the heavens will pass away with a loud noise, and the elements will be dissolved with fire, and the earth and everything that is done on it will be disclosed.' And in 3:13 he adds, 'But, in accordance with his promise, we wait for new heavens and a new earth, where righteousness is at home.' This is the fourth passage that we will look at in chapter 21.

Jude largely follows the same pattern as 2 Peter but has

nothing to say relevant to heaven except for the promise of
eternal life in verse 21, 'Keep yourselves in the love of God;
look forward to the mercy of our Lord Jesus Christ that
leads to eternal life.' But he does end with the lovely blessing that makes a fitting end to all the rest of the New
Testament before we turn our attention to the book of
Revelation – Jude 24–25, 'Now to him who is able to keep
you from falling, and to make you stand without blemish
in the presence of his glory with rejoicing, to the only God
our Saviour, through Jesus Christ our Lord, be glory,
majesty, power, and authority, before all time and now and
for ever. Amen.'

17

The Resurrection Body of Jesus

Before turning to the book of Revelation we will, as promised earlier, consider the resurrection body of Jesus and try to see what, if anything, it teaches us about the resurrection body of the redeemed.

As a lead in it may be appropriate, and make for completeness, to look at three other people who appear in the pages of the Bible after their deaths – Samuel, Moses and Elijah.

Samuel appears in the strange incident with the medium of Endor in 1 Samuel 28. A lot could be written about what exactly was going on in this encounter, but we will confine ourselves to things that describe the appearance of Samuel. In verse 13 the medium says, 'I see a divine being (or a god) coming up out of the ground.' This probably means ghost-like. And in verse 14 she further describes him as, 'An old man . . . wrapped in a robe.' In verses 15–19 Samuel makes it clear that he is not exactly pleased to have been disturbed in this way, and goes on to pronounce in no uncertain terms God's judgment on King Saul.

We may gather that prior to this Samuel had been 'sleeping' in Sheol, and we may gather that this kind of meddling with forbidden things will not achieve anything desirable, and most certainly will not alter the judgment of God; but regarding the resurrection body, it tells us nothing, this seems to be just a ghostly appearance of the old man as he was when he died.

What about Moses and Elijah on the mount of Transfiguration? (Matthew 17, Mark 9, and Luke 9) – A very different, but equally strange, encounter. This time we are given no description of them at all except that they talked and were presumably somehow recognisable. So we do not get much help there.

There is one other case in the Bible of people being seen after their death and that is in the account in Matthew 27:51–53, of some of the extraordinary things that accompanied those most extraordinary events of all – the death and resurrection of Jesus: 'At that moment the curtain of the temple was torn in two, from top to bottom. The earth shook, and the rocks were split. The tombs also were opened, and many bodies of the saints who had fallen asleep were raised. After his resurrection they came out of the tombs and entered the holy city and appeared to many.'

All very intriguing, but it tells us nothing of what they were like, and we need to be clear that with all these cases we are dealing with events before the day of judgment, and so before the start of the real life to come that we associate with heaven. None of these sightings can be said to be of someone in a final 'heavenly' body.

And so we turn to look at the one case that we may expect to teach us something more – Jesus himself.

Jesus has been crucified, officially certified as dead, embalmed and wrapped in burial cloths, placed in a rock hewn tomb and sealed in; but on the third day the tomb was open, the body was gone, but the burial cloths were still there and it sounds as though they were positioned as though the body had just passed through them. Then he begins to appear to the disciples.

There are all sorts of questions we might ask, such as: Where did the clothes he was now wearing come from? Where did the fish he had cooked, in John 21:9, come from? How could he be handled and eat food and yet appear in a room which had the doors locked? We have to say that we simply do not know, and it really doesn't matter.

The question that we must concentrate on is not, 'How?' but, 'What?' What was he like and does it teach us anything about what we will be like?

There are two main strands to what we are told. The first is that he was very solid and very real. He could be handled, he could cook fish, he could eat fish. The second is that he could appear inside a locked room and he could disappear out of their sight. In other words he seemed to behave very much like some of the angels we come across in the Old Testament.

Another significant thing we are shown is that he was the same but somehow different. He was not always recognised straight away. The strange nature of this is neatly expressed in John 21:12, 'Now none of the disciples dared ask him, "Who are you?" because they knew it was the Lord.'

What we would like to know is whether this body that Jesus had after the resurrection was similar to the resurrection bodies of the redeemed?

In some ways it seems to fit in with things we have gleaned from the Gospels and the Epistles: the same but different, a new body but with continuity with what we had before. However we need to be careful before we simply say that this is what we will be like, for we have to consider carefully what this body was for and whether it can be taken to be in any way the norm.

The point is that in the Gospels we see Christ's body as man on earth, and we are shown that he had a normal human body. In the book of Revelation we see highly symbolic pictures of the glorified Christ which are magnificent in what they teach, but have no resemblance whatever to his body as man. And thirdly we have the post resurrection body as described in the Gospels. This was the form he had between his resurrection and his ascension 'back home to heaven'.

What was this body for? One primary purpose was to prove that he had been raised from the dead, not as a spirit, but 'bodily'. This was not a ghostly appearance but a real flesh and bones appearance (see Luke 24:36–43). It had a very clear and precise purpose – to show the reality of the resurrection.

We have nothing that tells us directly what his 'body' is like after his ascension back to heaven, but there are possible hints to be found in the words of the angels at the Ascension, Acts 1:11 'Men of Galilee, why do you stand looking up towards heaven? This Jesus who has been taken up from you into heaven, will come in the same way as you saw him go into heaven.' This could certainly be taken as indicating that he still retains that body now, and will return with it at his second coming. And there is also the fact that when Stephen was being stoned to death he said, Acts 7:56 'I see the heavens opened and the Son of Man standing at the right hand of God!' How did he know that this was who he was? Presumably because he looked the same.

So we can make a strong case for saying that the resurrection body of Jesus gives us a good idea of what our resurrection bodies will be like. Spiritual and yet comfortingly similar to what we already know. Just as solid and real as our present physical bodies but not subject to the same limitations. Clearly his resurrection body was in several ways similar to that of angels, and as he said that we too will be like the angels, then it is logical to say that his resurrection body does indeed give us a good indication of what we will be like.

However we need to be careful, it is not quite as simple as that. It is not at all certain that this is the right way to understand it. We cannot say definitely whether this was a normal resurrection body or whether it was a unique body adopted for a unique purpose. He was, after all, a totally unique person. He became man for his life on earth, but there is nothing to say that he would necessarily remain in any way like a normal man after his death.

There are also big questions to be asked about age. Jesus died at the age of about 33–35, a man in the prime of life, but what do we think of people who die with their bodies worn out by the ravages of extreme old age, or what about little children. Are they to remain forever as very old, or very young? I have always thought, without any real justification, of the departed as being at the prime of life for ever, but if that is right some of them would be very different from how I last knew them. It may be relevant to note that angels always seem to be ageless, they are never described as young or old, and what would such a thing mean in an eternal life? In Daniel 7 God is described as 'the Ancient One' or 'the Ancient of Days' but that doesn't mean that he is an 'old God', it means that he has always been there. He himself is simply the I AM. He is not young or old, he just IS.

What I am getting at, is that if Jesus had died at a great age, or very young we might not find it nearly so easy to identify his resurrection body with what our spiritual bodies will be like. But perhaps this is all part of the wisdom of God, one of the reasons why Jesus had to die at the age that he did.

In some ways this chapter may seem unsatisfactory because it comes to no firm conclusions, but that may be the main point that needs to be made. I hope that it may cause some, who have a very simple belief that their bodies in heaven will be like Christ's resurrection body, to stop and think through some of the implications of such a belief. And also that it may cause others who disagree with that belief to see that it actually has a lot going for it. And finally that we may all realise that we will always be left with some unanswerable questions.

18

Introduction to the Book of Revelation

I believe Revelation to be a tremendous book, a priceless jewel that we neglect to our very great loss. I believe it to be as much inspired by God as any other part of the Bible, but it is different. It is the description of either one, or a series, of visions that show us things in picture form that take us beyond the edge of human comprehension. It has a certain likeness to some parts of the Old Testament prophetic books, especially Ezekiel, Daniel and Zechariah, but in its totality it stands out as unique in the Canon of Scripture. If it is to be compared with anything in the Gospels and the Epistles, it would be wise to compare it with the parables rather than with the direct teaching.

If the pictures in it are taken literally, they can become foolish and contradict each other, but if they are taken as divine pictures, something similar to the parables of Jesus, then they convey to us an impression of things that are beyond our normal capacity to understand. We are not worried by the fact that Jesus said the kingdom of heaven is like a grain of mustard seed, and like a net, and like a pearl, and like hidden treasure, and so on. We understand that these are all illustrations increasing our understanding of something that is greater than all of them put together.

Nor should we be worried by the fact that Revelation uses illustrations that seem mutually contradictory, but which properly understood increase our understanding of things greater than all of them put together.

It may be wise to re-state here something said earlier, namely that we must be consistent in how we treat the Bible. In particular it is not consistent to treat a particular passage as illustrative and then to pluck out a few words, or a few verses, from it and say that these bits are factual. Used in that kind of way we can make the Scriptures say almost anything we want them to say. It is a temptation to which many have fallen, but which we must resist.

As we look at the pictures of heaven, we should not think, 'but that's impossible.' As we might of gateways made out of gigantic pearls, and as we wonder where the gargantuan oysters came from that produced such pearls. Nor should we think, 'but that's ridiculous,' as we wonder at the description of a city that is said to be fifteen hundred miles long, wide, and high. Rather we are to be moved to wonder what it is really about, what the picture is saying to us, what it is pointing us to.

Some of the pictures in Revelation are gruesome, because they represent a terrible fate, but we are fortunate that our topic here is heaven, and so we only need to look at the pictures that are beautiful and awe inspiring. We will find that there are many echoes of the more concrete facts that we have seen in the Gospels and Epistles. It is almost as though what we have here is an appendix containing the illustrations that an artist might have inserted into the pages of the New Testament, except that no human artist could draw these pictures and so they have to be presented in words. John saw them in his visions, and he has been inspired to describe them, we must seek

God's inspiration to understand them.

Most readers will be aware that there are many different ways of interpreting its various parts. This is no new thing – in the early years of the church some of the prominent leaders, such as Saint Augustine of Hippo, began by holding to one way of interpretation but later changed their minds considerably.

We will endeavour not to get caught up with the details of possible different understandings of the various sections except where they have an obvious bearing on the topic of heaven, but we do well to be aware that apart from dealing with details, there are also major divisions of opinion on what the whole book is about.

Some think that it is all about life at the time that it was written, portraying the conflict between the church and the Roman Empire and that the pictures of the new Jerusalem and the new heaven and earth are about the new thing God is doing in this present age through his church. It is all seen as illustrating God's coming vindication of the persecuted church and the destruction of the persecuting Roman Empire.

We may well think that the church, as we know it, falls very far short of the perfection pointed to by these passages, but there are good reasons for giving this idea some serious consideration.

Firstly, if this idea is adopted then we are to realise that it is God's view we should consider and not man's view. When we look at ourselves, if we have any honesty, we would be bound to say that we are sinners, but when God looks at us he sees not our sins but the righteousness of Christ in which he has clothed us. And what is true of us as individuals is also true of the church, we may look at the church and see its many failings, but God sees it as the Bride of Christ.

Secondly, we can find several passages that would fit well into this concept. For example Paul says that Christians are the temple of God. He does not say that they will be one day, but that they are now. Hebrews 12:22 says, 'But you have come to Mount Zion and to the city of the living God, the heavenly Jerusalem . . .' He does not say they will one day come there, but that they are already there.

We may couple this with what is sometimes called 'now, but not yet' theology, which teaches that the Kingdom of God is already here but is not yet fully visible. One day it will be seen in all its fullness, but in this present time it is only manifested partially; and so Jesus said to his disciples, 'But if it is by the finger of God that I cast out the demons, then the kingdom of God has come to you.' (Luke 11:20). And, 'the kingdom of God is among you.' (Luke 17:21). But he also taught them to pray, 'Your kingdom come.' And he repeatedly spoke of the kingdom as something coming in the future.

Almost inevitably, there are points at which this scheme of understanding fails, for example both Paul and Peter were people living in the 'church age' but they were looking forward to something better to come. I say, almost inevitably, because it seems that any scheme that seeks to find an explanation in terms of something on this earth, fails at some point. Perhaps this is an indication that all such schemes are misled, or at the least, incomplete.

So this approach has quite a lot to commend it, but it has its weaknesses, and most scholars would say that it cannot be the complete answer for there are parts of Revelation which clearly speak about the very end of time as *we* understand it.

What this way of thinking can however do for us is to act

as a warning not to automatically think that something in the Book of Revelation is about heaven in the future when it may in fact be about something that already exists here and now.

If we were to embrace this particular way of understanding Revelation fully then the logical conclusion would be that there is very little in the book which could be said to be about heaven, which most people would think to be a most surprising conclusion.

In the next chapter we will be assuming that there are indeed things to be learnt about heaven, for the more usual approach is to consider that part of it is about the time of the Roman Empire but that it also looks ahead to all similar conflicts, right up to the final judgment and beyond. Within this framework there are many variations, in particular, some think there is a progression through history from start to end. (Not quite as simple as that maybe, but that's the general gist of it.) Others think that there are a series of visions which in their different ways overlap each other, each covering a span of history, though with an increasing emphasis on the last days as the Book progresses.

Which of these two approaches we adopt will have a considerable bearing on how we view topics dealing with earthly history and with subjects such as the millennium; but will not greatly affect the teaching about heaven.

My personal view is that Revelation is about both the present and the future and I am drawn to the idea of overlapping visions, each covering a span of history but with increasing emphasis on the end times and eternity as the Book progresses, but it is not my purpose to be dogmatic that this is necessarily correct.

So let us now turn to look at passages from the Book itself.

19

The Book of Revelation

First of all we have a series of glimpses of heaven in the promises given to 'those that conquer' at the end of the letters to the seven churches in chapters 2 – 3. These cryptic verses are not always easy to understand, but we can get a feel of the great glories and privileges that go with being in heaven.

2:7, 'To everyone who conquers, I will give permission to eat from the tree of life that is in the paradise of God.'

2:10, 'Be faithful until death, and I will give you the crown of life.'

2:17, 'To everyone who conquers I will give some of the hidden manna, and I will give a white stone, and on the white stone is written a new name that no one knows except the one who receives it.'

2:26–28, 'To everyone who conquers and continues to do my works to the end, I will give authority over the nations; to rule them with an iron rod, as when clay pots are shattered – even as I have received authority from my Father. To the one who conquers I will also give the morning star.'

3:5, 'If you conquer, you will be clothed like them in white robes, and I will not blot your name out of the book of life; I will confess your name before my Father and before his angels.'

3:12, 'If you conquer, I will make you a pillar in the temple of my God; you will never go out of it. I will write on you the name of my God, and the name of the city of my God, the new Jerusalem that comes down from my God out of heaven, and my own new name.'

3:21, 'To the one who conquers I will give a place with me on my throne, just as I myself conquered and sat down with my Father on his throne.'

We will be able to tie up at least four of the things mentioned in these verses, with things we have come across already. All of them in some way point to a special relationship with the glorified Jesus Christ, and we have seen time and again how central Jesus is to any understanding of heaven.

As we move further into this wonderful, but complex, book; it may be helpful to refer back to something else that Paul said in 2 Corinthians 12:2. He is describing the visionary experience of someone (himself), and says that this person was, 'caught up to the third heaven.' No one can be sure what Paul meant by that expression. One could easily understand a second heaven to mean God's dwelling place as opposed to the sky, but this is a third heaven. It might just be possible to understand Paul as saying, not just the sky, and not just space, but God's abode, but it is highly unlikely that he would have made this sort of distinction between the sky and space beyond it. It could be an abstract philosophical figure of speech, but it would be reasonable to think that Paul is speaking of there being different levels in heaven. If this is so it may help us to unravel some of the problems relating to things said to 'come down from God out of heaven' and yet which appear, in some ways of understanding it, to still be 'in heaven'.

And so it is that in 4:1 we are told that John, who appears to already be in heavenly realms, is called to, 'Come up here' and we find that he is in the presence of the throne of God and of God himself. There follows a highly symbolic description of what he saw there, and eventually to a description of the worship that is offered there. Perhaps the easiest parts to understand, are ultimately the most important, namely, the samples of the praise that is offered there: 4:8, 'Holy, holy, holy, the Lord God the Almighty, who was and is and is to come.' And, 4:11, 'You are worthy, our Lord and God, to receive glory and honour and power, for you created all things, and by your will they existed and were created.' One thing that we can learn from this chapter is that one of the main occupations in heaven will be praising God. We can safely say that no one who does not like praising God would be happy there.

The vision continues in chapter 5, and we come to the entrance of Jesus, well – he has been there all the time, but this is the first time John sees him in this particular vision, or this particular part of his vision. He is introduced with the words, 5:5, 'See, the Lion of the tribe of Judah, the Root of David, has conquered, so that he can open the scroll and its seven seals.' John looks to see this Lion, and what does he see? 5:6, 'Then I saw between the throne and the four living creatures and among the elders a Lamb standing as if it had been slaughtered.' What a complex but wonderful picture is presented to us, no wonder no one could actually paint it. The power of the Lion is demonstrated in him being slaughtered as the Lamb. This may not seem to be telling us much about heaven, but we find that it does, for it tells us how we can get there. This is expressed in the next song we hear being sung, 5:9, 'You are worthy to take the scroll and to open its seals, for you were slaughtered and by your blood you ransomed for God saints from every tribe and language and people and nation.'

In 5:12 Jesus is given a similar level of worship as was given to the Father in 4:11, and in 5:13 Father and Son are worshipped together, 'To the one seated on the throne and to the Lamb be blessing and honour and glory and might for ever and ever!' The point to be drawn from all this for our study is that Jesus Christ is absolutely central and pivotal to heaven and our place in it.

In chapter 7 we are shown who will be in heaven. Verses 7:5–8 show us twelve thousand being sealed from each of the twelve tribes of Israel. The number, twelve thousand, is highly symbolic and indicates not a mathematical number, but a full completeness. All from the Old Testament age who ought to be in heaven, will be in heaven. And then in 7:9 We are shown those from the New Testament age who will be there, 'After this I looked, and there was a great multitude that no one could count, from every nation, from all tribes and peoples and languages, standing before the throne and before the Lamb, robed in white, with palm branches in their hands.'

Here is a vast throng, for the invitation is to all, but they are clothed in white, representing that they have come the right way, that is, clothed in the righteousness of Christ. This is indicated in 7:14, 'they have washed their robes and made them white in the blood of the Lamb.' It is the fact that Jesus has died for them that means that their sins can be taken away and they can be clothed in his righteousness.

This is all leading up to a description of the bliss of those who are there in heaven: 7:15–17, 'For this reason they are before the throne of God, and worship him day and night within his temple, and the one who is seated on the throne will shelter them. They will hunger no more, and thirst no more; the sun will not strike them, nor any scorching heat; for the Lamb at the centre of the throne will be their shepherd, and he will guide them to springs of the water of life, and God will wipe away every tear from their eyes.' What wonderful word pictures we have here. The Lamb that was slain has become the great Shepherd of the sheep.

In this passage are echoes of some of the great Isaiah prophesies, which may suggest to us that we are not meant to find the final fulfilment of those prophecies on this earth, but in heaven. See Isaiah 49:10, 'they shall not hunger or thirst, neither scorching wind nor sun shall strike them down, for he who has pity on them will lead them, and by springs of water will guide them.' And, Isaiah 25:8, 'Then the Lord God will wipe away the tears from all faces.'

Chapter 14:1–5 speaks of one hundred and forty four thousand saints, it would be logical to take these to be the same hundred and forty four thousand (twelve thousand from each of the tribes of Israel) mentioned in 7:4–8. Here they are described as being, 14:4, 'redeemed from humankind as first fruits for God and the Lamb.' This fits in well with the idea that the first Christians in Israel were the first fruits of the harvest, to be followed by the full harvest of the great multitude that no one could count drawn from every nation on earth.

Verse 13 of chapter 14 would seem to be a word of comfort to those who have had a particularly hard journey through life, persecuted for their faith, but remaining faithful, 'And I heard a voice from heaven saying, "Write this: Blessed are the dead who from now on die in the Lord." "Yes," says the Spirit, "they will rest from their labours, for their deeds follow them."'

In 19:6–8 we come to something that has been hinted at in the Old Testament, in the Gospels and in the Epistles, the marriage of Christ to his church.

> Then I heard what seemed to be the voice of a great multitude, like the sound of many waters and like the sound of mighty thunder-peals, crying out, 'Hallelujah! For the Lord our God the Almighty reigns. Let us rejoice and exult and give him the glory, for the marriage of the Lamb has come, and his bride has made herself ready; to her it has been granted to be clothed with fine linen, bright and pure.'

There have been many who have wondered why Jesus did not marry. Some say that he did marry and have woven fantastical stories about it. Some have said that he ought to have married, and that his failure to do so has meant that some other religious leader has had to complete what he failed to do – just as fantastical. The truth of the matter is that it would have been totally inappropriate for Jesus to marry during his time on earth, for his destiny was to be 'married' to all his people. Using marriage as the deepest way of expressing total unity – what the Bible calls the 'one flesh' relationship. Here is the fulfilment of Christ's prayer in John 17:21–24,

... that they may all be one. As you, Father, are in me and I am
in you, may they also be in us, so that the world may believe
that you have sent me. The glory that you have given me I
have given them, so that they may be one, as we are one, I in
them and you in me, that they may become completely one, so
that the world may know that you have sent me and have
loved them even as you have loved me. Father, I desire that
those also, whom you have given me, may be with me where
I am, to see my glory, which you have given me because you
loved me before the foundation of the world.

This prayer has, of course, a fulfilment in this world. Jesus
is praying for the unity of his church, a prayer to which the
church has sadly often been somewhat deaf; but it also has
that connection with his people being with him in glory,
united with him in glory.

Chapter 20, strictly speaking has nothing about heaven.
It does however introduce 'the millennium' which we will
look at in the next chapter.

At last in 21:1–4 we read,

Then I saw a new heaven and a new earth; for the first heaven
and the first earth had passed away, and the sea was no more.
And I saw the holy city, the new Jerusalem, coming down out
of heaven from God, prepared as a bride adorned for her
husband. And I heard a loud voice from the throne saying,
'See, the home of God is among mortals. He will dwell with
them; they will be his peoples, and God himself will be with
them; he will wipe every tear from their eyes. Death will be no
more; mourning and crying and pain will be no more, for the
first things have passed away.'

And 21:6, 'To the thirsty I will give water as a gift from the
spring of the water of life.'

Many will have heard these words of comfort read at funerals and not realised that, as well as being comforting, they also present a puzzle. For at first sight it seems to speak of a new earth, with a new city, come down from heaven to earth. It seems to speak of God coming down to dwell with people on earth, rather than of people going to live with God in heaven. However the rather similar passage in 7:15–17 is clearly in the setting of heaven with the angels all around; and when we read on and come to the description of the new Jerusalem, we will realise that we are not dealing with anything like a city on earth. This is the last of the five passages we will look at in greater detail in chapter 21.

But now to look at the description of the new Jerusalem. The whole of chapter 21 ought to be read. The first thing to notice, something that can easily be missed, is 21:9, 'Come, I will show you the bride, the wife of the Lamb.' And what is he shown? He is shown, 21:10, 'the holy city Jerusalem coming down out of heaven from God.' If we take this too literally it is very odd. It has been made clear who are the bride of the Lamb, they are the people of God, so why is it a city? And how could a city ever be a bride? And yet, yes, there it is back at 21:2, 'And I saw the holy city, the new Jerusalem, coming down from heaven from God, prepared as a bride adorned for her husband.' What on earth is it about? Or perhaps I ought to ask, what in heaven is it about?

We look at the details we are given of the city and the mind boggles. It is here in 21:21 that we come across the twelve gates each made out of a single pearl. But there is far more than this. 21:16, 'The city lies foursquare, its length the same as its width; and he measured the city with his rod, fifteen hundred miles; its length and width and height are equal.'

It is worth asking how an angel with a measuring rod could, quite quickly it would seem, measure a city that is fifteen hundred miles long, wide and high; for this may act as a reminder that this is a picture of a reality, and not the reality itself. As I write this I have just come in from a five-and-a-half-mile walk. How do I know? Because I have measured it on the map (my picture), using a piece of string (my measuring rod).

The translation gives the measurement in miles, for otherwise it means nothing to us, but in so doing something is lost, for the original Greek has twelve thousand stadia, which is another of those symbolic numbers, meaning 'total fullness'. As a symbolic measure it is full of meaning as a literal measure it becomes almost grotesque. And now we must look at its shape – a perfect cube. This is not the only place we come across a perfect cube in the Bible. There is one other thing, and one other thing only, of which we are told that it has this shape, and that is the Holy of holies in the tabernacle and then in the temple. What we have here is a picture of the true Holy of holies, not a miniature representation in the tabernacle, or in the temple in Jerusalem, but the real thing – the holy dwelling place of God, which is his people, who are the bride of Christ. This 'City of God' is not a city made by God for people to live in, but a people made by God to be a dwelling place for him to live in. We have come across this before.

We could go on and look at all the details of the description, all the precious stones and the gold everywhere. No sun or moon, for God dwelling in the city is its light, and so on. But just when we may think we have begun to understand what it is about – the people of God as the temple in which God lives, we find our thoughts turned upside down, or inside out, as we read, 21:22, 'I saw no temple in the city, for its temple is the Lord God the Almighty and the Lamb.' And, as we read on into chapter 22 the picture begins to look much more like a place in which people dwell, with the river of the water of life flowing through it with the tree of life growing beside it. We might see this as all very confusing, but more positively we may see it as a picture of the two-way relationship we have come across earlier which we might summarise as 'I in them and they in me'.

But now, how is that bit in Revelation 20 about the thousand years, the millennium, meant to be understood? And how are we to take the bit about a new heaven and a new earth in Revelation 21?

Before entering the two 'diversions' for which we have seen warning signs, it may be important to take stock of what we have so far discovered. In particular to ask what we have heard about the nature of the future body and the place of the future abode. The overwhelming teaching so far about the future body is that it is to be a spiritual one, with the proviso that we realise that this means not something less real than our present body, but something far more real, substantial and lasting. And the overwhelming teaching so far about the place of the future abode is that it is to be in heaven, though what it will actually be like is still far from clear.

20

The Millennium – Diversion 1

Yes, it is time to take a look at the millennium. Whilst the different ideas regarding this may not be actually about heaven they do have a considerable bearing on the question of when the redeemed get there and what they may go through 'on the way'. Once we begin to look at the subject, we realise that we are driving into a horrendous 'traffic jam'. There are many widely differing ideas regarding it, and each of the main ideas has spawned numerous sub-divisions.

As we go into this chapter, I would urge you not to forget that part of the journey we have already travelled, what we have seen from all the rest of the Bible. We must maintain a proper balance and recognise that while a traffic jam may consume a disproportionate amount of time on a journey, it is to be hoped that it is only a short part of the total journey, and it is most definitely not the final destination.

The foundation for everything to do with the millennium is Revelation 20:1–10, 'Then I saw an angel coming down from heaven, holding in his hand the key to the bottomless pit and a great chain. He seized the dragon, that ancient serpent, who is the Devil and Satan, and bound him for a thousand years, and threw him into the pit, and locked and sealed it over him, so that he would deceive the nations no more, until the thousand years were ended. After that he must be let out for a little while.

Then I saw thrones, and those seated on them were given authority to judge. I also saw the souls of those who had been beheaded for their testimony to Jesus and for the word of God. They had not worshipped the beast or its image and had not received its mark on their foreheads or their hands. They came to life and reigned with Christ for a thousand years. (The rest of the dead did not come to life until the thousand years were ended.) This is the first resurrection. Blessed and holy are those who share in the first resurrection. Over these the second death has no power, but they will be priests of God and of Christ, and they will reign with him for a thousand years.

When the thousand years are ended, Satan will be released from his prison and will come out to deceive the nations at the four corners of the earth, Gog and Magog, in order to gather them for battle; they are as numerous as the sands of the sea. They marched up over the breadth of the earth and surrounded the camp of the saints and the beloved city. And fire came down from heaven and consumed them. And the devil who had deceived them was thrown into the lake of fire and sulphur, where the beast and the false prophet were, and they will be tormented day and night for ever and ever.'

At first I hoped that I might be able to drive straight through this 'traffic jam' with my eyes shut! To just ignore the whole issue because it becomes so complicated. I reluctantly realised that this was neither honest nor satisfactory. Far too many people hold to one or other of these ideas for it to be simply ignored, and their ideas inevitably affect their view of the ultimate destiny of the saved, and especially the question of when do they get to heaven. My second line of approach was to look at all the main ideas assuming a neutral position, trying to present each idea impartially. I eventually realised that this too was neither honest nor satisfactory. It was not satisfactory because it became so long and complex that there was a danger of it overwhelming the whole subject of heaven, undermining the attempt to hold all the Bible has to say on the subject in balance. It was also bordering on dishonesty because I was presenting ideas as though they had biblical support, when I really thought that some at least were profoundly unbiblical, which was hardly right in a book which is meant to be 'a biblical exploration'.

Anyone who wishes to look into these ideas will have to look elsewhere, searching under titles such as: eschatology, millennium, tribulation, rapture, dispensationalism and a host of other related topics, though I would personally advise great caution, for it is all too easy to be led away into an alien, almost fairy tale like landscape, far removed from the teaching of Jesus and the apostles. In particular some things to be found on the internet have no scholarly basis and can be quite horrendous, with statements along the lines of 'I have met with God and he has told me . . .' followed by highly dubious statements. It might not be so bad except that you can then find another web site making similar claims but with quite different statements. Beware! Taking God's name in vain is alive and well on the internet!

My thinking on this subject eventually led me to the conclusion that as there are so many conflicting schemes about the millennium centring on this one passage, and as all but one of them must be wrong, there is therefore a strong probability that they are all wrong. And that, as so many of them must be wrong, there must be a suspicion that the passage of Scripture on which they are based does not provide an adequate foundation for what has been built upon it. Or, to put it more bluntly, that those verses are being unwittingly misused.

In my earlier years I gained a degree in Civil Engineering and worked for some years as a civil engineer. One of the lessons I have always carried with me from that time is the peril of building anything on an inadequate foundation, so it was only natural that it was in this direction that I found my thoughts turning. Are these ideas built on a firm biblical foundation?

If we read through the Bible from start to finish looking for references to the millennium, or any kind of reference to a period of a thousand years, we will have a very fruitless search. There is no such reference in the whole of the Old Testament, nor in the Gospels or Acts, nor in all the epistles except for one reference in 2 Peter 3:8 which addresses the problem of promises of God not being fulfilled as soon as expected by saying, 'But do not ignore this one fact, beloved, that with the Lord one day is like a thousand years, and a thousand years are like one day.' We can notice in passing that this is not speaking of a literal period of time, but simply making the point that God's view of time is different from ours, it is simply a contrasting of a long time with a short time.

We then continue to read on and find no other references until we come to those in Revelation 20:1–10, and then that's it. There are no more. Nor incidentally are there any references to it in the Apocrypha, or as far as I can find, in any other writings known to have been around at the time of Jesus and the Apostles.

If there were some references in the Old Testament and the rest of the New Testament, or if there was even one, we might say, 'God has prepared us for this.' But there are none. We therefore need to approach the Revelation 20 passage with great care. We need to ask, 'What sort of a passage is this? What is its context? How does it fit in with the rest of the Book? What is it really about?' Just to take those few verses and make them the foundation for a whole plan of history is an extremely dubious thing to do. Let's look at those four questions in order.

'What sort of a passage is this?' Well, the vast majority of the Book of Revelation is clearly visionary. 1:10, 'I was in the spirit on the Lord's day.' describes the nature of John's experience. As we read the Book we repeatedly come across things that taken literally become grotesque but taken as pictures, or illustrations, are magnificent. The overwhelming probability is therefore that this passage, 20:1–10, is also meant to be taken as a picture or illustration. It could be literal but the nature of the whole book makes that very unlikely.

'What is its context?' The passage that immediately precedes it is clearly very symbolic. Whilst parts of the following section could be taken literally, other parts cannot. And within itself are parts that must surely be taken as a picture, for example we are unlikely to think that we are meant to take literally the part about the devil being chained with a great chain and thrown into a bottomless pit which is then locked and sealed; rather this is a magnificent picture of the power of the devil being restrained. So the context points strongly to things that need to be taken pictorially.

'*How does it fit in with the rest of the book?*' The real question of course is, 'What is the book for?' It is God's message, through his servant John, to people who have put their faith in a Lord who they believed had won the victory over sin and death, and over all the powers of evil, but find that they are suffering terribly for that faith. Their anguished cry is, 'Why, and for how long?' The whole book can be seen as a series of pictures that in their different ways give the message that the enemy's power is coming to an end and is as nothing compared with the total victory that God has won in Jesus Christ. They are to hold fast to the end and they will enter into an eternity of glory. It would therefore be very reasonable to expect this passage to fit in with that general pattern.

So, '*What is it really about?*' Without wanting to be dogmatic about it, I would suggest that the context of the whole book in general, and of its immediate location in particular, and also its own internal content, point to it being one more way in which God is impressing on his persecuted people that the power of evil is as nothing compared with the almighty power of God. This is not future history, or even any kind of history at all, but divine illustration. Jesus was forever telling parables and using illustrations, and the book of Revelation follows the same pattern.

What I would say more dogmatically is that the whole context and pattern of the book makes these verses an inadequate foundation on which to build any literal timescale. They have no Old Testament foundation, no Gospel foundation and no apostolic foundation; and they provide an inadequate foundation within themselves. We would do well to sidestep all systems of belief that rely too heavily on this one passage. Far better to be comforted by one more illustration of the all-surpassing power and victory of God and of the sure and certain reward of the persecuted martyrs, than to build great edifices on a foundation that cannot bear their weight. It is true that some of the systems built on this foundation do not take the thousand years to necessarily mean an exact thousand years, but rather a long period of time, but this makes little difference to the general criticism, and in fact shows an ambivalent attitude – it this passage literal or not?

I am well aware that there will be many who will accuse me of trivialising the millennial positions, and who will point to supposedly supporting passages from Ezekiel and Daniel (some of which we have looked at earlier) and will find supporting verses in the Gospels and Epistles. My reply would be that it is not my wish to denigrate the integrity of those who think differently on this, but to simply assert that while there are these other verses that could possibly be made to fit into a millennial scheme, they do not provide sufficiently strong support. The millennial schemes would never have been thought of if Revelation 20 was not taken literally, and this, as I have endeavoured to show, is a very dubious line to take.

I would like to emphasise here that I am not claiming that I am necessarily right in my views of this, but I am claiming that the foundation for these ideas is very shaky, and I am urging that they be considered with the greatest caution. My concern is that ideas built on such an insubstantial foundation must not be allowed to change the way we view the more straightforward teaching of Jesus and the Apostles and the rest of the Bible in general. That more straightforward teaching is that after death we 'sleep' in Sheol/Hades until Jesus comes again, when we will go to be with him for ever; and Jesus tells us that he will come to take us to be with him in his Father's house. Any teaching that would interpose another period of something quite different seems to me to be unnecessary, unhelpful and unwarranted.

While you may (or may not) think that by examining the foundation of all the many millennial theories I found a way round a major traffic jam; there is another major detour we still need to investigate. The next chapter of Revelation, chapter 21, presents us with some challenges which, as I understand it, turn out to be about the question of: 'Is it a matter of heaven on earth, or heaven like earth?'

21

Heaven on Earth? – Diversion 2

When, a few years ago my wife and I toured New Zealand by car, there was one leg of our journey where the road had been blocked by a major mud slide and we had to take a complex diversion. Part of the route used what British drivers would consider to be a not yet completed road through the mountains with just a wet mud surface. For me, as driver, it was really quite scary; but because of this diversion we came across what we came to look upon as our favourite place in the South Island. My experience as I researched this chapter was somewhat similar; my initial sense of confusion as I grappled with a group of passages that seemed to disagree with what I was increasingly certain was the teaching of all the rest of the Bible was eventually to give way to delight at finding that they led me to unexpected treasure. I was to find that they did not have to be seen as disagreeing with the rest of the teaching, but that they could be seen as adding important extra insights to it. They draw out teaching that cannot be found elsewhere, and our exploration would be incomplete without them.

There is however no quick and easy way through these passages, for though they have the unifying thread of things relating to a new, or renewed, earth; yet they also contain considerable internal differences; but I urge you not to be put off, for the 'slippery road' (going back to my New Zealand road illustration) is well worth the effort.

Before looking at the passages we can do something to reduce the complication by rejecting two possible approaches. It is not an option simply to ignore them. Nor is it an option to say that they must be taken illustratively without saying what it is that they illustrate. Each of these approaches would be a misuse of Scripture.

This leaves us with two possible main ways of seeing them, the first is to take them very literally, which can lead to the idea that our final destiny is not in heaven but on a literal renewed earth. The other is to take them illustratively but to seek for a clear understanding of what it is that they are illustrating – what new insights they give us, and lead us into. With this introduction let us turn to look at the five passages.

Revelation 21 starts with the verse, 'Then I saw a new heaven and a new earth; for the first heaven and the first earth had passed away, and the sea was no more.' So here is the lead in to the idea that the final destiny of the redeemed is not to be in 'heaven' as it is normally understood, but to be on a new and perfect earth, or an earth restored to its original perfection before the fall.

We will immediately realise that this is one of those places where the use of the word 'heaven' is very problematic. We are looking at the whole subject of what we normally call 'heaven', but in this verse the word translated as heaven most likely means the sky. However, in the second verse we read, 'And I saw the holy city, the new Jerusalem, coming down from heaven from God, prepared as a bride adorned for her husband.' What 'heaven' is this?

It could mean the sky or it could mean God's abode. We could say that there is a measure of ambiguity built into these verses. Whatever else they are, they are not entirely straightforward. They need careful study.

Some of the millennial ideas, put in a simplified form, suggest that the redeemed will rule over the earth for a time before it is 'wrapped up' and they are transferred to heaven. But that is not what we will be concerned with here. Here we are looking at the idea that the redeemed will have an eternal life on a new, or restored earth. This is what I have called, 'heaven on earth'. The idea is not that people will go to live with God in heaven, but that God will come to live with people on earth. This is an idea that is particularly attractive to some of those who have a highly developed ecological concern, some of whom take it very literally and argue that Christians have a particular duty to preserve this earth because they will live on it for ever. Nothing that I say against this view should be taken to be against ecological concerns themselves which can be argued more than adequately from other Bible passages. However I have to say at the start that I find it difficult to see how a concept of a literal time and place bound heaven on earth can be made to tie up with John 14:1–6 and John 17:24, and a whole host of other key verses, but it is a concept that we need to consider seriously, for we have already seen the two way paradox of 'us in God' and 'God in us', so who is to say that there is necessarily any conflict between 'heaven on earth' and 'earth in heaven'?

It is important to notice the fundamental difference between the topic of this second diversion and that of the first diversion: unlike the millennium, Revelation 21:1 does not 'appear out of nowhere', there are things in both the Old and New Testaments that prepare the way for it, notably those four passages: Isaiah 65:17–25, Acts 3:19–21, Romans 8:18–23 and 2 Peter 3:13. So let us look at these four passages and then come back to Revelation 21 itself.

Isaiah 65:17–20,

> For I am about to create new heavens and a new earth; the former things shall not be remembered or come to mind. But be glad and rejoice for ever in what I am creating; for I am about to create Jerusalem as a joy, and its people as a delight. I will rejoice in Jerusalem, and delight in my people; no more shall the sound of weeping be heard in it, or the cry of distress. No more shall there be in it an infant that lives but a few days, or an old person who does not live out a lifetime; for one who dies at a hundred years will be considered a youth, and one who falls short of a hundred will be considered accursed.

The passage continues on into the well-known idyllic description of the wolf and the lamb feeding together.

The initial fulfilment of this prophecy was to do with the return of the people of Israel from captivity in Babylon and the rebuilding of Jerusalem, but it is clearly about more than just that. It holds out the promise of a perfection that was never fulfilled at that time, nor ever since, and which we could only imagine being fulfilled in some form of existence that is completely different from that which we know at present.

We may note two things about this prophecy. Firstly, it brings together the creation of new heavens and a new earth, with the creation of a new Jerusalem. We will need to bear this in mind when we look at Revelation 21. We will need to look at the two things together and not treat them in quite different ways.

Secondly, though it may well give a lead into a later fulfilment that embraces the concept of eternal life, of itself it is not about eternal life, but about people living out a mortal lifespan, up to a hundred years maybe, but still mortal.

Next we turn to Acts 3:19–21, Peter is speaking to the crowd that has gathered after he and John had been used by God to heal the lame man at the Beautiful Gate of the temple, he says,

> Repent therefore, and turn to God so that your sins may be wiped out, so that times of refreshing may come from the presence of the Lord, and that he may send the Messiah appointed for you, that is, Jesus, who must remain in heaven until the time of universal restoration that God announced long ago through his holy prophets.

What are these 'times of refreshing' and more particularly this 'universal restoration'? The prophets had repeatedly promised that if the people would repent and return to God, God would bless them, but the promise of universal restoration seems to refer particularly to that promise in Isaiah 65, in which case Peter is pointing ahead to another greater and more complete fulfilment still to come.

This leads us to Romans 8:18–23,

> I consider that the sufferings of this present time are not worth comparing with the glory about to be revealed to us. For the creation waits with eager longing for the revealing of the children of God; for the creation was subjected to futility, not of its own will but by the will of the one who subjected it, in hope that the creation itself will be set free from its bondage to decay and will obtain the freedom of the glory of the children of God. We know that the whole creation has been groaning in labour pains until now; and not only the creation, but we ourselves,

who have the first fruits of the Spirit, groan inwardly while we wait for adoption, the redemption of our bodies.

That's quite a passage! Commentators have had many and varied ideas about how it is to be understood. Briefly I would suggest that Paul is saying that when Adam and Eve first sinned and as part of the consequence God had said to Adam, Genesis 3:17–18, 'cursed is the ground because of you; in toil you shall eat of it all the days of your life; thorns and thistles it shall bring forth for you.' He, God, had always had in mind that one day the curse would be removed and that the whole of creation would benefit from the great restoration. And so, Paul is saying, 'Wait for it. Look forward to it. It will be tremendous. It will not be just the redeemed that will be blessed, it will be the whole of creation.' Whether we take this literally or illustratively it widens our view of what is involved in our redemption. In some way or other it affects more than just people, it affects the whole of creation.

And finally we have the passage in 2 Peter 3. The writer has been saying that this earth as we know it 'is reserved for fire' (verse 7), and 'the elements will melt with fire' (verse 12), and then he says, 2 Peter 3:13, 'But, in accordance with his promise, we wait for new heavens and a new earth, where righteousness is at home.' So whether the writer is Peter or someone else, and there are arguments about that, he agrees with Peter in Acts and Paul in Romans. There is a great day coming when God will do something tremendous that will involve the whole of creation and establish a new creation, or a renewed creation, in which his purposes can be fulfilled without the taints of sin. The question we face in this chapter is, to what extent is this a literal renewal of this present world, or to what extent is it a picture of something beyond our experience, something even greater, and if so, what does it teach us?

So we come back to Revelation 21:1, 'Then I saw a new heaven and a new earth; for the first heaven and the first earth had passed away, and the sea was no more.' Those last six words may alert us to something that ought to be obvious: this is certainly not a re-creation of anything like the earth created in Genesis 1, where the sea plays a vital role. Perhaps we need to be reminded that this is still all part of a visionary experience in which the sea is seen as a symbol of division and of untamed forces.

Next we need to be consistent and see that verses 1 and 2 go together, 'Then I saw a new heaven and a new earth . . . And I saw the holy city . . .' And as we look at the description of that new Jerusalem, as we have done earlier, we soon realise that it is a picture of a reality, not the reality itself. So to be consistent we have to say that the new heaven and new earth is also a picture of a reality, not the reality itself.

Thirdly we need to note that there is no further description given of this new heaven and earth, all the description that follows is of the new Jerusalem, and is clearly symbolic. If we want to build up a possible description we have to go back to the other references. A place where righteousness is at home, well that is to be expected but it doesn't tell us anything physical. Wolves and lambs feeding together, the lion eating straw like the ox; we could take this literally, but most people take it as a picture of perfection, and in Isaiah 65 it is actually about Jerusalem not the world outside, (65:25).

There may be differences of opinion on this, but I would humbly suggest that it is impossible to take this teaching totally literally without doing violence to the text, and without it being so much in conflict with other clear teaching that we would have to reject, or ignore, much of that teaching, something I personally could not do. So it seems to me that we have to take them as illustrative, but what exactly is it that they illustrate? I believe they point us to tremendous truths.

I personally found that it was thinking about the description of heaven as a 'new earth' that began to bring my thinking about heaven 'down to earth', and to see how it all fits in. Nowhere else in all of Scripture do we find much that really helps us with the question of what heaven will be like, in the sense if what it will 'look like'. The descriptions we do find, for example in the book of Revelation, are gloriously metaphorical, they tell us to some extent about the values and activities of heaven, but not what it actually looks like, and we can therefore easily find ourselves making up our own imaginary heaven. The human mind is wonderfully fertile and can dream up all sorts of strange and wonderful ideas, which may in fact be very misleading and unhelpful, and so there is a very real need for our thinking to be brought 'down to earth'.

We have already concluded that the spiritual body is to be understood to be very real and solid, these verses encourage us to apply that same thinking to the spiritual realm (heaven) in which the spiritual body will live. We have in fact come across pointers to this before, for example Hebrews 11:13–16.

These verses also suggest that when we think of heaven, not only should we not think of some vague ethereal existence, but that nor should we try to dream up some totally different kind of creation, but that we should think in terms of what we already know, namely the earth on which we now live. Not meaning that it will be exactly the same, but that the nearest we can get to understanding it is to think in earthly terms. We would be well advised to think of everything we have known in, and of, this world, that has been good, and to say that heaven will be like that but better.

Perhaps we should think along the lines of the place that God has prepared for us in the heavenly realms being made to be very like this earth; so much so that it can be called a 'new heaven and a new earth'. This would give us a 'home from home' as it were; but in reality it would be this world that is the 'home from home', and our place in heaven which will be our real home.

Others may want to go further than this and say that there are therefore good grounds for saying that somehow something of this present physical world will be taken up into heaven. This would be similar to what we already believe about ourselves, extending to the 'new earth' what we have been shown to be true of the 'new body'.

And so this diversion leads us to the fundamental proposition that we are to think of heaven in terms of what we have already experienced of God's ways on this earth. Once we have grasped this principle it can help us in our thinking about a number of questions to which we have so far found no clear scriptural answers.

As an example we may start with the question of whether in heaven we will meet and know loved ones from the past. This we can largely answer from other places, such as the teaching that love never ends, and even the final verse of the unusual parable of the unjust steward, Luke 16:1–9, could be taken to encourage us to expect a continuation of relationships into eternity. These passages that we have looked at in this chapter would certainly strengthen such an understanding, but now to extend that question to something that no other passages say anything about.

Can this idea be extended to include that much-loved pet? And will there be any place for animals in heaven?

When God created animals he thought he had done a good thing (Genesis 1:21) and there are a number of places where God says unexpected things about animals, for example what are we to make of the last verse of Jonah? However when everything else in the Bible is put together we can only get as far as saying that we can't be certain if they have any place in the life to come. But when we look at the question from the basis of heaven being thought of in earthly terms the balance shifts considerably, and it is possible to argue that it would be very unlikely that the God who filled this earth with such a magnificent variety of living creatures, would be content with a new creation containing only angelic beings and redeemed people. Perhaps Isaiah 11:6–9 and Isaiah 65:25 ought to be taken a bit more literally than I seem so far to have allowed, and as we have just seen, this would fit in more easily with Romans 8:18–23. So will we meet that much-loved pet in heaven? I really don't know, but I certainly wouldn't rule it out, and in fact on the basis of these passages I would be inclined to expect that we will.

At this point you might well accuse me of drifting towards a more literal understanding of these passages. In one way this would be true, but in another way, not at all. Yes, I am suggesting that we need to think of heaven in terms of the illustrations we are given. I suggest that we might well imagine that when we get to heaven we will find ourselves thinking, 'I seem to know this, I have the feeling that I have been here before, it is just like (some favourite place) but better.' However this new place in which we will live is not to be seen as being literally on this earth as it is, for we are told plainly that it will be consumed; nor is it to be seen as on any kind of physical planet at all, for the fate of all such planets is eventually to die or to be consumed, whereas the heavenly realm is eternal. Paul is very emphatic about this difference between the physical and the spiritual.

The right balance seems to be that we are not to take these verses as being literally about this earth renewed, or of any other kind of physical earth, they are illustrative of the spiritual realm we generally call heaven; but in the context of that spiritual realm, heaven, they are to be understood not as vague illustrations, but as something nearer to being literally true. Heaven is being presented to us not as something strange and alien, but as something familiar and friendly, something that we can, within the limitations of our little minds, begin to actually visualise.

So these passages, which can cause problems when people take them over-literally and particularly when they treat them as though they are the sum total of all the teaching about the life to come, can, when integrated in with the other teaching, add a whole new 'dimension' to our thinking, and lead us to the very comforting conclusion that we will not find heaven to be something frighteningly alien, but something reassuringly familiar. What seems certain is that we can only think sensibly of heaven in terms of what we already know and experience.

One way of summing all this up might be to say that if we think of heaven as being a new and perfect earth, we may not be strictly speaking correct, but nor will we be far wrong. Or another way of summing it up might be to simply say that our thinking about heaven needs to be very firmly earthed.

22

Conclusions

There is almost always something more that can be found in the Bible on any subject but we have now come to the end of all the main teaching on the subject, our exploration is over, and so we come back to our five questions: Where? What? When? Who? and How? Can we summarise some conclusions? Some answers are clear, some will still be beyond us, for we are dealing with things beyond the borderline of our ability to understand. There is as little chance of us ever understanding some of these things in this life, as there is of a dog trying to understand how a computer works; our understanding may not get far beyond that of the poor dog wagging his tail. However God has told us enough for us to have at least some glimpses of the truth.

Where?

The question, 'Where?' has been largely answered in the previous chapter. Heaven will be in – well – in heaven; in other words in the heavenly realms where God dwells; but we will not be far off the mark if we think of it in very earthly terms.

Of course we would love to know more. We speak of it

as up, but we know that this is only a figure of speech. Good things are thought of as up and bad things are down. We don't try to locate heaven in some specific physical position, for we know that spiritual 'geography' is different from that of this world in which we now live. When it comes to the point our physical minds can only work on a physical level and so can only understand heavenly things by means of physical illustrations, hence all the parables and the pictures in the book of Revelation.

Where it is, is really of little importance for Jesus has promised that he will take us there, so we can leave that to him. Far more important is the question, 'What is it?'

What?

And now we must try to sort out what is the meaning behind all those illustrations and pictures. We will realise that God would not have used all these pictures if the explanation was one that we could easily understand. In trying to understand it we may be trying to do what God has indicated we are in fact incapable of doing. Well – let's see how far we can get.

For simplicity I will from now on speak of heaven as a 'place', for though it might be more correct to think of it as being a 'place or state of existence', for it is not part of physical geography as we understand it, yet we can only think of it meaningfully in terms of what we already know. All Jesus' parables were firmly rooted in things to do with this earth on which we now live.

Heaven is a place that is characterised by faith, hope and love. It is a place of worship. It is a place of absolute purity and holiness. It is a place of joy. It is a place of life. In it there appear to be different levels, with different levels of rewards and differing levels of service. This should not be seen as being against those of lesser ability, but rather as being of great comfort to everyone of whatever ability – there will be a suitable place and occupation for all to enjoy at the level of their own unique ability and disposition.

Heaven is where God dwells. It is where Jesus dwells. It is where the Holy Spirit dwells. To be there is worth more than anything else. It is a place where all who are there are secure, with their own special position, and yet all are one.

Its occupants are like the angels, they have spiritual bodies, but these spiritual bodies must be understood to be much more solid and real than our present physical bodies, they are almost certainly recognisably who they were in their life on earth, though quite how is not explained for we will be ageless. It may be significant that Jesus was in the prime of life at his death and resurrection. There are good grounds for believing that we will meet and know our loved ones from the past, together with all the redeemed that we have known.

When we turn to look at the pictures in the book of Revelation, we find that the relationship between the new Jerusalem and heaven is problematic. On the one hand it comes down out of heaven from God, but on the other hand it is the heavenly city, and God dwells in it, and God is its temple; and yet again it is a picture of the people of God in whom God dwells.

The dimensions of the city, a perfect cube, indicate that it is the true Holy of holies, the place where God dwells, that it is made of pure gold indicates that it is absolutely holy. Here we see a picture of Paul's teaching that Christian people are the Temple of God.

So from one viewpoint, the new Jerusalem is the people of God in whom God dwells. But from another viewpoint, the new Jerusalem is the Father's house, in which the people of God live, and as such it has the river of the water of life flowing through it and the tree of life growing beside it. What we have here is a very complex picture that speaks of a two-way relationship. We are here very near to the two-way relationships expressed by Jesus in his great prayer in John 17, and there are other passages in the Epistles that speak on the one hand of 'being in Christ', and on the other hand of 'Christ in you'.

This all speaks to us of almost total unity with God. As we go on to consider this further, and find that we will be like God (1 John 3:2), and that we will sit on God's throne (Revelation 3:21), and that we will be married to Christ; we may fear that we are in danger of becoming blasphemous. I suggest that here is another reason why God has spoken to us in pictures: that the straightforward truth is not only beyond our ability to understand, but may also be, better, higher, more glorious, than we are as yet able to accept. All we can really say is that it will be right and it will be perfect, but with the added points that it will also be purposeful and most definitely it will be fun, otherwise, what is the point of all the pictures and stories about banquets and feasts. Finally, the verses we considered in chapter 21 would suggest to us that we will actually find it to be comfortingly familiar rather than frighteningly alien. (For a fuller treatment of this see the last thirteen paragraphs of chapter 21.)

When?

When do people who are going to heaven, actually get there? The answer seems to be straightforward, but needs one bit of clarification.

The simple answer is that it will be when Jesus Christ comes again, when we are told that, 1 Thessalonians 4:16–17, 'the dead in Christ will rise first. Then we who are alive, who are left, will be caught up in the clouds together with them to meet the Lord in the air; and so we will be with the Lord for ever.' In other words, this will be at the day of resurrection for those that have died, and at the second coming for those who are still alive.

The teaching of both the Old and New Testaments is that between death and the day when Christ returns, people are in Hades, the place, or state, of the departed. Clarification is needed because Paul says he longs to depart and be with Christ, making it sound as though he will be with Christ instantly. How are we to make that agree?

The general way of speaking in the Bible of those who have died is to say that they are sleeping. This comes in both Old and New Testaments. But it is clear that some are sleeping in peace, while others are sleeping in fear of the judgment. We could perhaps think in terms of sweet dreams, or nightmares. And the nature of the sweet dreams for the redeemed is that they are with the Lord. This could possibly tie in with some so-called near death experiences.

Another possibility is that while, in terms of this life, there may be a long period between death and the day of resurrection, at death we actually step out of time, and the next thing we know we are directly at that great day.

There may be other possibilities, and it is really impossible for us to know, but the practical point is that, for the redeemed, the experiences after death will all be wonderful. In one way or another, we will be with the Lord for ever.

This may be satisfactory from a theological point of view, but when someone has been bereaved they are likely to approach the subject from a rather different angle, asking, 'Are my loved ones, who loved Jesus, now with Jesus, and have they now received their new spiritual bodies?' They are not interested in the general theory, but in the personal details relating to their loved ones. It may be helpful to take a second look at these questions from this more personal and pastoral viewpoint.

So, are they now with Jesus and have they received their new spiritual bodies? I would suggest that the only balanced answer is a cautious, 'Yes and no.'

'Yes', they have gone to be with the Lord, but they are 'sleeping' until the day of resurrection, and so technically, 'No', they have not yet received their new spiritual bodies; that comes at that day of resurrection.

However, whatever exactly is meant by time after death, the next thing they can be expected to experience is the resurrection in their new spiritual bodies, when Christ comes again; so that it will probably seem to them that they have stepped straight from death to being with the Lord in their spiritual bodies.

As far as we are concerned, we are still very much living in this world, subject to the limitations of time that go with it. For us that day of resurrection has not yet come and so, in our relationship with them, our loved ones are still sleeping and have not yet received their new spiritual bodies.

All a bit complex, but we are dealing with two different forms of existence, that run parallel but do not really overlap. I suggest that it is perfectly permissible to think of a loved one who has died as being released from the limitations of their old bodies, but this release has been into the future with Christ at the resurrection and not into a new life that runs parallel with ours back here on earth.

We may perhaps think of them as having already got to the day of resurrection, and yet when we get there we will find that we arrive there together.

There is not meant to be any contact between those living on this world with its timescale, and those sleeping in 'Hades' with its different kind of existence. The only case we are given in the Bible of someone seemingly contacting the dead is that of King Saul contacting Samuel. We cannot be sure what exactly was going on here, but it is of interest to notice that what the medium supposedly saw was 'an old man', 'wrapped in a robe', who, as mentioned in Chapter 17, was not exactly pleased with being disturbed in this way. This was not Samuel in a new spiritual body but Samuel as he had been when he died. Whatever exactly was going on in this strange experience it was certainly very unsatisfactory, and something not to be copied.

On a much more harmless level: because we have talked regularly with a loved one for many years, when they die we may find that without thinking what we are doing we sometimes continue to 'talk to them'. This is not a crime, but nor is it reality. We are in fact talking to a 'memory', which is probably just another way of saying that we are talking to ourselves, and it is best to move as quickly as possible to talking to someone who really does hear, meaning, talking to God who is always ready to hear. The loved one could never be said to be at rest, or at peace, if they were actually still involved in the things of this life, and could hear our 'talking'. We say that we believe they are at peace, and we need to 'leave them in peace'.

The day will come when we will be together with the Lord for ever. We cannot bring that time forward however much we might wish to, and have to wait in faith, and with patience, for that day to come. To try to break through the boundaries before then by any means whatever would not only be wrong, but if it could be done, could destroy the joy of that great day when it comes.

Who?

And now we get personal. Who will go to heaven? It would be nice to think that everyone will eventually get there (or would it?). Whatever exactly we may think of that, what we find in the Bible are some massive qualifications that are needed.

We may look first at the qualifications dictated by the nature of heaven. It is a place of holiness and purity; a place of faith, hope and love; a place of worship; a place where God's will is done.

Then we can look at what is actually said of those that will be there. They will be people who are humble; people who have been forgiven and who forgive others; people who have been born again, or adopted into God's family.

Thirdly we can get more than a hint that it will only be for those who have thought it worth their while to strive towards it.

Fourthly we are told that there is only one way, and that is by Jesus Christ; and we have seen that Jesus is very central to most of the teaching about heaven.

Finally, we generally stop reading Revelation 21 at verse 7; but if we read on we are told very clearly the sort of people that will not be there, 'But as for the cowardly, the faithless, the polluted, the murderers, the fornicators, the sorcerers, the idolaters, and all liars, their place will be in the lake that burns with fire and sulphur, which is the second death.' (Revelation 21:8)

We are aware that Jesus said, Luke 12:32, 'Do not be

afraid, little flock, for it is your Father's good pleasure to give you the kingdom.' And when we hear the necessary qualifications, we will not be surprised that it is a 'little flock'. Indeed, we may well wonder whether it will be anyone at all, and yet we are told in Revelation 7:9 of 'a great multitude that no one could count'.

We face a quandary. We realise that heaven would cease to be heaven if the 'wrong type of people' were allowed in; but how can anyone qualify as being one of the 'right kind of people'?

A hint to the answer is already contained in some of the qualifications, namely the forgiven who have been adopted into God's family. We must now look at this more carefully.

How?

How can anyone ever make the grade? How can you or I be part of heaven? The short answer is, 'By grace.' This is what Christianity is all about, Jesus Christ doing for us what we could not do for ourselves. For a longer answer I reproduce here an extract from my previous book.

> How can this be? If God is utterly holy and if we are all sinners, how can we stand before him and not be consumed?
>
> The first thing to say is that God made us, and no matter how far we have fallen from being 'in his image', he still loves us, and he longs for us to return to what we ought to be. His attitude towards us is clearly shown in Jesus' parable of the prodigal son in Luke 15.
>
> The second thing to say is that we ourselves can never do what is needed to put right what has gone wrong. There is something wrong in us that makes this impossible. We only have to try to live a perfect life to find out that we can't.

The third thing to say is that because God loves us, and because he knows we cannot do it, he has stepped into our world to do it for us. This he did in Jesus Christ, who, without going into the deep theology of it, was God become man. The heart of what he did is expressed by John 3:16, 'For God so loved the world that he gave his only Son, so that everyone who believes in him may not perish but may have eternal life.'

We don't have to understand the full details. It is important that we try to understand it as best we can but we don't have to. All we need to do is to believe that Jesus died for us and that when he was crucified, he was in some way dying for our sin. He was doing what we could not do so that our sins could be forgiven. Not just glossed over, but totally dealt with and removed.

The fourth thing to say is that there is something we have to do. We have to accept what he has done for us. He did not do something mechanical for machines, he did something personal for people. We have to come to him and in some meaningful way express our regret for where we have gone wrong, ask for his forgiveness, and receive it as a gift.

And the fifth thing to say is that the consequences are immense and eternal. When we turn to Christ in faith there are two sides to what happens; on the one hand our sins are taken away. As far as God is concerned it is as if we had never committed them; and on the other hand we are 'clothed with the righteousness of Christ', meaning that when God looks at us he does not see us as sinners, nor even as sinners who have been forgiven, but as righteous because the Spirit of Christ, the righteous one, is in us. This is what makes it possible for us to come into the presence of God at the judgment and to survive, and far more than survive, to be part of his glory for ever. (*All You Need to Know About Hell*, Chapter 18)

Some may object that this is all too exclusive, and they may have taken exception to Christ's words in John 14:6, 'No one comes to the Father except through me.' It needs to be made clear that this is not saying that people can only come by belonging to a particular church. It is at least possible that some, or even many, who have not belonged to a church, or even thought of themselves as Christians, will, when they come face-to-face with Jesus, recognise the one for whom they have been seeking. It is of interest that many members of other faiths become Christians after they have had a vision of Jesus. They have been seeking for something, someone, and when they 'meet' him, they recognise him and accept him. It would be hard to believe that when such a seeking soul comes face to face with the living Christ at the final judgment, they will not accept him, and he will not accept them. Some such idea would be entirely agreeable with Christ's words, 'no one comes to the Father except through me.'

There is a danger that this kind of thinking can lead some to say that it doesn't matter what you believe, nothing could be further from the truth – this is about people who are earnestly seeking, not about people who are carelessly drifting; and what a shame to miss out on companionship with Jesus Christ in this life as well as in the life to come; and without a body of Christians on earth in this life, how are others to know that there is such a person as Jesus Christ for them to seek and to find?

To conclude let me quote some words from a famous Confession of Faith, 'The chief end of man is to glorify God and to enjoy him for ever.' It will be glorious and full of overflowing joy. Jesus calls us to come, let us seek him till we find him. Once we have found him, we will enjoy him, and he will enjoy us, for ever.

23

All You Need to Know?

Some may query whether this little book lives up to its name, *All You Need to Know About Heaven*. I believe it does, almost certainly a great deal more than anyone actually needs to know; but supposing I am wrong. Here is one word that will fulfil that claim – 'Jesus'.

If we know Jesus we need know nothing else. He came from there, he returned there, and he reigns there. He opened the way to go there, he will take us there, and he will welcome us there. We can leave everything else to him. Our speculations may sometimes be wrong, but he always does what is right, and will do for all eternity.

What do we need to know? Jesus. That is all, and that is everything.

The words of the chorus of a hymn written by Edward Mote (c. 1834) seem to sum up nicely the difference between what is certain and other matters we have considered that are by no means so certain:

On Christ, the solid rock, I stand –
All other ground is sinking sand.

EPILOGUE

'I'll Do It'

Some time later, Tom had another dream. He was standing in the middle of something that seemed like a very large dome, but whether or not there was a roof above he could not tell. What he did know was that all along one side he could see out onto beautiful scenery with attractive and well-kept paths, and with pleasant resting places at frequent intervals. He was tempted to wander out and enjoy it all, it would be so easy, so restful, and so undemanding.

But something held him back. There was something about it that made him feel uneasy. He couldn't quite decide what it was, but the words 'chocolate box picture' came to mind. It seemed to be artificially perfect and different in the wrong sort of way, there was something almost alien about it. Was it real?

And then there was that door on the other side of the dome. It wasn't particularly attractive but it looked very real and normal, and somehow familiar. It had some sort of notice on it and he thought he ought at least to see what it said. As he approached it he looked back and it seemed to him that the beautiful scenery was beginning to fade.

He was now near enough to read the notice on the door. It simply said, 'Come to Me.' The nearer he came, the more

137

attractive that simple door, that he now felt sure he had come across before, seemed to become.

He was right by it now and he realised with surprise that it seemed to be the door to his own home, but he knew that it was more than that, it was also someone else's home. 'Come to Me.' Who was 'Me'? He thought he knew. He thought it was someone he had been learning more and more about. He knew that it must be – and that the notice was a personal one addressed to him. It put into simple words a call, of which he had at first been only dimly aware but which had become increasingly clear in recent months.

He took a final look back but the scenery had vanished completely. In its place was something he could only describe as 'emptiness'. For a moment he wondered whether to go back and see if the beauty would return. He thought it probably would, but he realised that he wouldn't trust it even if it did; what would happen if he got caught up in something that wasn't real? But this door he felt was very real, and as for this 'Me', he realised that he had been longing to meet him for quite some time.

There was a final short hesitation and then he said in a determined voice, 'I'll do it.' He grabbed the handle, opened the door, and stepped through. Through into a brightness that amazed him, into a peace that engulfed him, into arms that enfolded him, and into a future beyond comprehension. He knew that he had 'come home' to where he wanted to be for ever.

*   *   *

In the morning his wife said to him, 'What was that all about?'

'What do you mean?' he asked.

'In your sleep you called out, "I'll do it." And then you slept like a log the whole night through. I haven't known you to sleep so well for years.'

'Well dear,' he said, and he set out to tell her what he had been doing over the past months and the conclusions he had been coming to, and how his dream had shown him the way he must go.

Being a wise woman she didn't say that she already knew most of what he told her. Week after week as she dusted the bookcase she had noticed that the Bible regularly changed its position and was beginning to look quite dog-eared. From little things he said she thought she had understood the nature of his quest, and she had seen a change growing in him, but she had thought it best to wait till he spoke about it before making any comment. Now that it had all come out into the open she felt a great sense of relief and expectation as she simply asked if she could join him in what he wanted to do.

And so it was that with some trepidation Tom and his wife arranged to see their vicar, and found not the forbidding character he had feared, but a warm and welcoming person who rejoiced in all Tom had to say. The kindly man arranged to help them on things they had not understood and with a number of unanswered questions; and within a year Tom and his wife were able to declare their faith publicly as they were confirmed in their village church.

It was not long after, that Tom fell seriously ill, and no treatment could cure his complaint. Some of his friends from earlier days were puzzled at how well he took it. He was the same Tom they used to know, and yet there was something different about him. He was concerned for his wife, but for himself, well, it almost seemed as though he was looking forward to something exciting. He talked about 'going home' with a twinkle in his eye.

The end came quickly. The family were gathered round the bedside. It wasn't a pleasant time, there was all the usual laboured breathing, but through it all Tom seemed more relaxed than many had expected. At the end they fancied that he tried to mutter something and then was clearly seen to smile, and he was gone.

Others wondered what he had been trying to say, and were glad that he had a 'peaceful death'; but his wife knew better than they, for she had heard his words clearly, 'I'll do it.' And she had seen more than just a smile, she had seen something she knew well, his smile of recognition; and though nothing could take away the grief of her loss, she was deeply comforted. 'My dear,' she said to herself, 'I'll do it, too.'